Blackstone's Guide to the
ASYLUM AND IMMIGRATION ACT 1996

Blackstone's Guide to the

ASYLUM AND IMMIGRATION ACT 1996

Leonard H. Leigh

Professor of Criminal Law at the London School of Economics

and

Chaloka Beyani

Lecturer in International Law and Human Rights
at the London School of Economics

BLACKSTONE
PRESS LIMITED

First published in Great Britain 1996 by Blackstone Press Limited,
9–15 Aldine Street, London W12 8AW. Telephone 0181–740 2277

ISBN: 1 85431 591 9

British Library Cataloguing in Publication Data
A CIP catalogue record for this book is available from the British Library.

Typeset by Style Photosetting Ltd, Mayfield, East Sussex
Printed by Livesey Ltd, Shrewsbury, Shropshire

Contents

Preface

Immigration law continues to be a major concern for Western governments and, in Britain, is in a state of constant flux. The Asylum and Immigration Act 1996 represents an attempt to tighten the net of control which surrounds those who come in search of asylum and it takes its place in a bundle of Western European measures initiated to the same end.

The resulting law is complex. The Act both amends procedures and creates new offences and in the process, significantly amends earlier legislation. It also affects the social security entitlements of would-be asylum seekers. This book is an attempt to explain the provisions of the Act and certain related legislation for the benefit of those who work in the field. It is not concerned to criticise policy: that is for another forum. We hope that it will prove helpful.

We express our thanks to all those at Blackstone Press whose efforts ensured the timely appearance of this Guide.

Leonard Leigh
Chaloka Beyani
November, 1996.

Commentary

INTRODUCTION

This Guide examines the content of the Asylum and Immigration Act 1996 (the 1996 Act) which is being brought into force by a succession of statutory instruments. At the time of writing the Asylum and Immigration Act (Commencement No. 1) Order (SI 1996 No. 2053 (c. 46)) has intimated commencement dates. These are specified in the schedule to the statutory instrument reproduced in this Guide.

As a result the new procedure rules are in force and so too are the rules concerning the removal of asylum claimants to safe third countries and the appeal procedures which relate to them. By the time of publication the criminal offence provisions of the new Act should also be in force. It is anticipated that another commencement order will shortly be made.

For the purpose of the Guide, it is vital to note that the 1996 Act is not a self-contained piece of legislation. Its format is largely in the form of amendments which supplement administrative measures for dealing with asylum and immigration, as contained in the Immigration Act 1971 as well as the Asylum and Immigration Appeals Act 1993. The 1996 Act clearly adds to the complexity of the existing law on the subject of asylum and immigration in the United Kingdom. For that reason, this Guide reprints not only the 1996 Act but also certain legislation which precedes it and, in particular, the 1993 Act with consolidated amendments.

The Guide begins by outlining the purpose for which the 1996 Act was enacted. It then provides the background to the Act and includes, in this regard, important legal developments at the level of the European Union in whose light the 1996 Act ought to be seen. Finally, the Guide examines the main heads of the 1996 Act, namely: the handling of Asylum claims as stipulated in sections 1–3 of the Act; the regime of Immigration offences established by sections 4–7 of the Act; and the restriction of immigrants to employment, and their entitlement to housing accommodation and assistance, and child benefit. Wherever appropriate, these matters are examined in the light of the international obligations of the United Kingdom towards refugees and asylum seekers. The reason for doing so is that upon introducing the 1996 Act the government announced its determination to honour the United Kingdom's obligations under the United Nations Convention Relating to the Status of Refugees 1951, and the Convention Against Torture, Cruel, Inhuman or Degrading Treatment 1981.

THE PURPOSES OF THE 1996 ACT

The purposes of this Act were set out as follows by the Home Secretary, the Rt Honourable Michael Howard, at the second reading of the Asylum and Immigration Bill in the House of Commons: (See Hansard, 11 December 1995, col. 699):

> The Bill has three objectives: first, to strengthen our asylum procedures so that bogus claims and appeals can be dealt with more quickly; secondly, to combat immigration racketeering through stronger powers, new offences and higher penalties; and, thirdly, to reduce economic incentives which attract people to come to this country in breach of our immigration laws.

These purposes show that the Act introduces contentious administrative measures designed to restrict severely the entry of asylum seekers, refugees, and immigrants into the United Kingdom under the guise of expediting 'bogus claims', combating 'immigration racketeering' and 'breach of immigration laws' by economic migrants.

Therefore, the 1996 Act is intended to extend the 'fast track' special appeal procedure, provided by the Asylum and Immigration Appeals Act 1993 (c. 23), to cases where the Home Secretary proposes to remove a person to a safe third country, and to allow the Home Secretary to designate selected countries as not giving rise to a serious risk of persecution.

In addition, the Act is aimed at enabling the imposition of limits on the right of a refused asylum seeker to appeal against deportation; and to provide fresh offences and enhanced penalties against what are perceived to be fraudulent asylum and immigration applications. Not the least contentious aspect of the Act is the obligations which it places on employers to ensure that persons offered employment are lawfully within this country.

The 1996 Act further imposes restrictions on access to social security benefits on the part of persons who arrive in Britain but whose claim for asylum is made at a later time. This aspect of the Act proved to be hotly disputed during the debate on the Bill in the House of Commons and had, at one time, to be withdrawn for consideration.

BACKGROUND TO THE 1996 ACT

The official account leading to the enactment of the 1996 Act points in the direction of a large increase in bogus claims for asylum in the United Kingdom. In truth, the 1996 Act is part of a network of pieces of legislation adopted by member states of the European Union to tighten immigration controls in the 1990's. When the Home Secretary, then Rt Honourable Kenneth Baker, first introduced the Asylum and Immigration Bill in 1991 (later to become the 1993 Act), he took the position that:

> Throughout Europe the institution of Asylum is under severe strain from the numbers using it as a way around immigration controls . . . From previous experience fewer than a quarter will be genuine refugees . . . I am therefore introducing a Bill and associated rules to streamline the processing of claims. The Bill provides a safeguard for genuine refugees by ensuring that all those refused asylum will have a right of appeal before removal and that points of law can be taken to the Court of Appeal. It will enable those without a proper claim to be dealt with more rapidly and effectively.

A web of treaties concluded within the framework of the agenda to establish free movement within the European Union pursuant to the Single European Act 1986 sets mutually reinforcing obligations for member states to restrict the entry of immigrants and asylum seekers into the European Union. The Convention applying the Schengen Agreement 1990 carries provisions which enable control of entry at the external borders of the European Union by means of visa and computerised exchange of information.

Reinforcing the Schengen Agreement are certain provisions of the Maastricht treaty on the European Union regarding uniform control of entry by means of entry visas, and which makes further provision for determining the third countries whose nationals must be in possession of a visa upon crossing the external borders of member states (Art. 100 C(1)(3)). Amongst the fields of common action determined by this treaty to be of interest to Member states are immigration, asylum policy, rules governing the crossing of external borders, and policy with regard to third country nationals (Art. K 1).

With particular reference to asylum seekers, the Convention Determining the State Responsible for Examining Applications for Asylum lodged in one of the European Communities 1990 determines, as its title indicates, the state which is responsible for examining an initial request for asylum. This Convention is not yet in force, but it is virtually applied by several member states of the European Union.

It is the substance of these treaties, taken together with similar legislation passed by other member states of the European Union, notably Germany and France, which provide a suitable background to the 1996 Act. The officially professed policy behind the Act is to grant entry, without further obstacle, to applicants who are genuine asylum seekers whilst effectively sifting out those who are not. The difficulty, however, is that like the 1993 Act before it, the 1996 Act inherently fails to distinguish between asylum seekers and refugees on the one hand, and economic migrants on the other.

In keeping with the spirit of the Dublin Convention, the 1996 Act implements the first country of asylum policy under which an asylum seeker should apply for asylum to the first safe country which he or she reaches. In effect, this policy restricts the claim for asylum to such a country, without scope for a claimant to present their claim to the United Kingdom.

A combined objective of the Dublin Convention and the first country of asylum practice is to prevent the irregular movements of asylum seekers and their circulation between countries. In implementing the first country of asylum policy, the Dublin Convention seeks to resolve the problem of orbiting asylum seekers by assigning responsibility to determine the status of asylum seekers. That way, states would not avoid their obligations to receive asylum seekers and to determine their status by floating them from one state to another.

The motives behind the 1996 Act appear to differ from these objectives. According to the Home Secretary, a significant underlying part of the 1996 Act would appear to address his or her concern that asylum seekers should not be able to pick and choose their preferred country of asylum. However, in mitigation to this stand, the Home Secretary undertook, in Committee, to take account of claims by those who already have close family ties within the United Kingdom (Standing Committee D, cols 283).

There is a danger that the underlying philosophy of the 1996 Act is likely to reinforce the trend of irregular movements and the avoidance of international obligations to determine the status of asylum seekers. The restrictive features of the 1996 Act will apply to those who do not come directly to the United Kingdom and the 1996 Act applies, in this regard, the third safe country practice at two levels. First, an asylum seeker who arrives in the United Kingdom via a safe country may be returned to such a country. In the second place, an asylum seeker may be sent to a safe third country instead of being offered asylum in the United Kingdom. And there is the restrictive requirement for unsuccessful claimants to appeal from abroad, and the refusal to give suspensive effect to appeals.

ASYLUM CLAIMS

In order to claim asylum successfully, an applicant has to show that the claim has a basis under the 1951 Convention. Article 1(2) of the Convention, read together with the 1967 Protocol to the Convention, establishes the basis for determining refugee status by reference to the following definition of a refugee as a person who,

> owing to well-founded fear of persecution for reasons of race, religion, nationality, membership of a particular social group or political opinion, is outside the country of his or her nationality and is unable or, owing to such fear, is unwilling to avail himself or herself of the protection of that country; or who, not having a nationality and being outside the country of his or her former habitual residence as a result of such events, is unable or, owing to such fear, is unwilling to return to it.

A claim for asylum based on the Convention has to show a well-founded fear of persecution on the grounds stipulated in the Convention and the burden of proof lies upon the applicant. The test applicable to establish a well-founded fear of persecution under the 1951 Convention was laid down by the House of Lords in the case of *R* v *Secretary of State for the Home Department, ex parte Sivakumaran* [1988] 1 All ER 193. See also *R* v *Secretary of State for the Home Department, ex parte Sandralingam and Ravichandran, The Times,* 30 October 1995. It was held in this case that the requirement in Art. 1(A)(2) of the Convention that an applicant for refugee status had to have a 'well-founded fear' of persecution meant that there had to be demonstrated a reasonable likelihood that he or she would be so persecuted. The Court stated that in deciding whether the applicants had made out their claim that their fear of persecution was well founded, the Secretary of State could take into account facts and circumstances known to him or established to his or her satisfaction, but possibly unknown to the applicant in order to determine whether the applicant's fear was objectively justified. This test has been applied to the handling of asylum claims in certain aspects of the appeal procedure under the 1996 Act.

The appeal procedure

Central to the 1996 Act is the extension of an accelerated procedure to cases compendiously referred to as 'claims without foundation'. In relation to such cases, section 1 of the Act substitutes a new para. 5 to schedule 2 of the Immigration Act 1993. The effect is to exclude these cases from appeals to the Immigration and Appeals Tribunal under part II of the Immigration Act 1971, and to provide instead for appeals to a special adjudicator (schedule 2, para. 5(7)).

The accelerated appeal procedure will take effect after an individual claim has first been considered by the Home Office and classified as falling within the class of 'claims without foundation'. Under Section 5(3) of the 1993 Act, an asylum claim is 'without foundation' if it does not raise any issue as to the United Kingdom's obligations under the 1951 Convention, or it is otherwise frivolous and vexatious. The case of *R* v *Secretary of State, ex parte Mehari and Others* [1994] QB 474 held that the true construction of the phrase 'without foundation' is that an appellant's claim does not raise any issue as to the United Kingdom's convention obligations unless on the facts it is incumbent upon the Secretary of State to consider his or her substantive claim to refugee status.

Other cases which also fall within the accelerated procedure include manifestly fraudulent or frivolous claims. An aid to the interpretation of such claims can be found in the conclusions drawn by the executive committee of the United Nations High Commissioner for Refugees (the High Commissioner), regarding its mandate and its supervisory responsibility for the performance of obligations under the 1951 Convention.

Under the statute establishing the mandate of the High Commissioner, 'manifestly unfounded claims' are those so obviously without foundation as not to merit full examination at every level of procedure. The conclusion (No. 30, xxxiv) adopted by the High Commissioner is that applications which have been termed either clearly abusive or manifestly unfounded are to be defined as those which are clearly fraudulent or not related to the criteria for granting refugee status laid down in the 1951 Convention nor to any other criteria justifying the granting of asylum.

In substance, 'claims without foundation', 'manifestly unfounded claims' and 'manifestly fraudulent or frivolous claims' are to be determined by reference to the extent to which they are related to the 1951 Convention, or other basis, such as the existence of the risk of torture in the country of origin (see below under appeals). The case for handling claims of this nature expeditiously under an accelerated procedure appears justified on two fronts. First, in order to protect genuine asylum seekers from others who do not have a well-founded fear of persecution, but who seek to gain entry through the facility of asylum; secondly, to avoid clogging the system of processing objective asylum applications, which in turn would ensure that genuine applications are dealt with as quickly as possible. The point of great concern is to eliminate any possible overzealous resort to the accelerated procedure as a measure of general immigration control of genuine asylum seekers.

Because of the amendments made by the 1996 Act, the accelerated procedure now applies, in summary, in the following cases:

(a) if the country or territory to which the appellant is sent is designated in an order made by the Home Secretary by statutory instrument as one in which it appears to him that there is in general no serious risk of persecution (the designated list or, colloquially, the 'White List') schedule 2, para. 2);

(b) if, on his or her arrival in the United Kingdom the appellant was required to produce a valid passport and either failed to do so without giving a proper explanation for his or her failure to do so or he produced a passport which was not in fact valid and failed to inform the officer of that fact (schedule 2, para. 3(a) and (b));

(c) if the claim does not show a fear of persecution by reason of the appellant's race, religion, nationality, membership of a particular social group, or political opinion (schedule 2, para. 4(a));

(d) if the claim shows a fear of such persecution, but the fear is manifestly unfounded or the circumstances which give rise to the fear no longer subsist (schedule 2, para. 4(b));

(e) if the claim is made at any time after the appellant has been refused leave to enter under the Immigration Act 1971, or has been recommended for deportation by a court competent to do so, or has been notified of the Home Secretary's decision to make a deportation order against him or her by virtue of section 3(5) of that Act (the general deportation provisions which include deportation on grounds of public good) or has been notified of his or her liability to removal under schedule 2, para. 9 of that Act (the removal of an illegal entrant) (schedule 2, para. 4(c)(i)(iv));

(f) if the claim is manifestly fraudulent or any of the evidence adduced in its support is manifestly false (schedule 2, para. 4(d)); or

(g) if the claim is frivolous or vexatious (schedule 2, para. 4(e)).

The purpose of these provisions is to accelerate appeal procedures in order to check the flow of individuals who the government believes to be abusing the asylum procedures, either by claiming asylum in a country other than the first country of asylum to which the claimant comes or because the true ground of the claim is not persecution, but it is, for example, economic in character.

A claimant may contend either that he has personally been the object of persecution or that he or she belongs to a group which has been persecuted. The accelerated procedure will apply if the claimant's application, based on either of the above contentions, is or appears to the Home Office not to show a fear of persecution on any Convention ground or if it shows a fear of persecution which is manifestly unfounded, or if the circumstances which give rise to the fear no longer exist. Claims which are apparently economic in nature will thus fail under either of the three grounds just mentioned, unless, indeed, it can be shown that a government is using economic deprivation as a weapon against a particular group or person. Fraudulent claims also fall under the procedure provided that they are manifestly fraudulent.

In order to avoid the fast-track procedure the applicant must give a clear indication of a fear of persecution on the relevant grounds. The claimant must therefore show that his or her claim has a Convention basis. It would seem (to take a case raised in standing committee) that a person who seeks asylum because he or she is being persecuted by particular social, political or religious groups within his or her country will have to show, if the accelerated procedure is to be avoided, a measure of state action by the country of origin, whether by way of active encouragement or passive connivance on the part of that state's authorities.

If a claim is made on Convention grounds, but certified by the Home Secretary as fit for the accelerated procedure, it will follow that the government considers that there is no serious risk of persecution in the designated country. That country may be his or her country of origin or it may be a third state from whence the applicant arrived in the United Kingdom. In respect of the designation of a country, whether or not it be the applicant's country of origin, the test applied by the Home Secretary is whether there is in general a serious risk of persecution. This test would appear to differ in quality from that of 'a well-founded fear of persecution' under the Convention. However, designation will give rise to a rebuttable presumption that a claim from a national of a designated country is unfounded. The list may be added to, or subtracted from, by order provided that such an order prevails. The first designation order requires an affirmative resolution of both Houses of Parliament, but thereafter the negative resolution procedure applies (schedule 2, para 5(8)). The remedy for inappropriate designation must, therefore, be Parliamentary.

It would seem that (as earlier noted) Western European countries have been working to a broadly common list of such countries since 1986–1987 when they held intergovernmental consultations outside the institutional framework of the United High Commissioner for Refugees. Thus in 1990, Poland, Bulgaria, Algeria, and India were listed as safe countries. Others considered were Romania, Bangladesh, Morocco, Tunisia, Ghana and Egypt.

Countries are dealt with as a whole. Thus a country may fall within the list even though there appears to be persecution in some specific part of it. In the government's view people should, if they are able to do so, seek safety in safe areas of their own country, the 'internal flight principle' which is internationally recognised if not a principle of international law.

The fact that countries placed on the White List are dealt with as a whole avoids the individual assessment of asylum claims and raises an issue of lack of compliance with the criteria established under Art. 1 of the Convention Relating to the Status of Refugees under which the existence of a well-founded fear of persecution has to be established on an individual basis. There is no requirement under the Convention, or in international law, that persons should be able to seek safety in safe areas of their own country under the so-called 'internal flight principle'.

The holistic designation of countries as safe 'in general' aroused disquiet in Parliament. It is certainly indefinite in character and its conformity to international standards applicable to individual asylum seekers is highly questionable. However, its purport was explained by the Home Secretary as follows:

> . . . designation will not amount to a declaration that we necessarily consider countries to be universally safe, or to have political and judicial institutions that function to western standards. We could not possibly accept an obligation to apply such standards and no such obligation exists in international law. What we will be saying is that a country has functioning institutions and stability and pluralism in sufficient measure to support an assessment that, in general, people living there are not at risk.

It should, however, be emphasised that the extension of the accelerated appeal procedure is not intended to preclude individual consideration of cases from individuals arriving from designated countries. Such individuals will still be able to present such claims and in some cases may, in any event, be given exceptional leave to remain. But there is no doubt the new procedure disfavours applicants from designated countries.

The cases which the government proposes to catch under (e) and (f) above include the following (Standing Committee D, 16 January 1996, col. 139):

(a)   claims based on facts that differ from and are wholly incompatible with those cited by the applicant, whether in a previous claim, in contact with the authorities, or in the same application;

(b)   repeat claims on identical facts which have already been refused; and

(c)   multiple applications in several identities.

In all cases the applicant will have come from so-called safe countries.

It is, however, the evidence in support of the claim for asylum which must be manifestly false. The expressed intention is not to penalise individuals who have had to travel on false papers since refugees as a practical matter must often do so. Thus a claim will not be allocated to the fast-track procedure simply because the claimant on arrival in this country admits that his or her exit papers or passport are false. At the same time, the government places very great importance on the applicant showing candour on first arrival in this country.

The government thus noted that although those who withhold, conceal or destroy papers usually do so for the following reasons:

> Some wish to conceal the fact that they travelled on their own passport, since this may give the lie to their claim that they are being sought by the authorities in their own countries. Some wish to conceal the fact, which their passport would reveal, that they have travelled here from a safe third country, in which they could have sought asylum. Others try to conceal their true identity or nationality. At the end of the day it is considerably more difficult to effect the removal of someone who is without travel documents.

The government therefore expects candour and the legislation reflects this (HL Deb. vol. 571, col. 1122 per Baroness Blatch). The practice remains to be seen. However, in terms of the United Kingdom's international obligations, Art. 31 of the Convention Relating to the Status of Refugees prohibits the imposition of penalties for illegal entry or presence on refugees who come directly from a territory where their life or freedom was threatened, provided they present themselves without delay to the authorities and show good cause for their illegal entry or presence.

Late claims

The late claims procedure (under schedule 2, para. 4(c)) will not apply to claimants merely because they fail to apply at the point of entry. It applies to those who make a claim when they are told that they are liable to deportation or removal as an illegal immigrant or by order of a court following a criminal conviction. Claims of this character were identified as constituting a major abuse of the system of asylum, and immigration control.

If a claim falls within subparagraphs (2), (3) or (4) of para. 5, no appeal lies by the appellant to the Immigration Appeal Tribunal. There are, however, two cases in which appeal to the Tribunal is unaffected. The first is where evidence adduced in support of a claim for asylum establishes a reasonable likelihood that the applicant has been tortured in the country or territory to which he or she is to be sent (schedule 2, para. 5(5)). This part of the Act reflects certain obligations contained under the Convention Against Torture and Other Cruel, Inhuman or Degrading Treatment or Punishment, 1984 to which the United Kingdom is a state party. Article 3 of this Convention prohibits the expulsion, return ('refoulement') or extradition of a person to another state where there are substantial grounds for believing that he or she would be in danger of being subjected to torture.

For the purpose of the Convention, the term 'torture' means any act by which severe pain or suffering, whether physical or mental, is intentionally inflicted on a person for such purposes as obtaining from him or a third person information or a confession, punishing him or her for an act he or a third person has committed or is suspected of having committed, or intimidating or coercing him or a third person, or for any reason based on discrimination of any kind, when such pain or suffering is inflicted by or at the instigation of or with the consent or acquiescence of a public official or other person acting in an official capacity. It does not include pain or suffering arising only from, inherent in, or incidental to, lawful sanctions.

For the purpose of determining whether substantial grounds exist for believing that a person would be in danger of being subjected to torture if expelled, returned ('refouled') or extradited to another state, Art. 3(2) of the Convention Against Torture obliges the competent authorities (in this case the Home Office) to take into account all relevant considerations including, where applicable, the existence in the State concerned of a consistent pattern of gross, flagrant or mass violations of human rights. (See the decision of the Committee Against Torture in the case of *Mutombo* v *Switzerland* CAT/C/12/S/13/1993. The jurisprudence of the European Court of Human Rights under Art. 3 of the European Convention on Human Rights is to the same effect e.g. *Soering* v *UK* (1989) ECHR, Ser. A, 161. It will be noted that the burden of proof lies upon the applicant who need not strictly prove that he was tortured in that place, but must raise a reasonable likelihood of being tortured. It is submitted that the single most weighty factor is likely to be convincing medical and/or psychiatric evidence of torture. The requirement of a likelihood that torture occurred in the particular country could not, surely, require proof with the same strictness. A person's scars may be readily visible; a country's torture chambers may not.

The second is where the special adjudicator believes that the certificate was wrongly issued, but that asylum should be denied anyway. In both these cases the claimant will be able to appeal to the tribunal. The Crown's right of appeal is, in any event, unaffected by these changes.

REMOVAL OF ASYLUM CLAIMANTS

Section 2 of the 1996 Act permits the removal of an asylum claimant from the United Kingdom, notwithstanding certain protections from removal in both the Immigration Acts of 1971 and 1993. Such a person may be removed if the Secretary of State certifies that certain conditions, adumbrated below, are fulfilled, if the certificate has not been set aside on appeal, and except in the case of a person who is to be sent to a European Union country or a designated state, if the time for giving notice of such an appeal has expired and no appeal is pending (section 2(1)(a)–(c)). It will be seen that where the claimant is to be removed to a European Union country or a designated state a notice of appeal will not have suspensive effect (section 2(3)). This point is dealt with more fully below.

The relevant conditions are that the person is not a national or citizen of the country or territory to which he is to be sent; that his or her life and liberty would not be threatened in that country or territory by reason of his or her race, religion, nationality, membership of a particular social group or political opinion; and that the government of that country or territory would not send him or her to another country or territory otherwise than in accordance with the Convention.

It is not, however, the case that the claimant need have any connection with the designated State to which he or she is to be sent. The criteria essentially relate to two matters. The first is that the state is an appropriate state, that is, in general, the first safe country to which the asylum seeker came. Such a state may be entirely foreign to the claimant. The second is that the designated state will respect the doctrine of 'non-refoulement' according to which it will not send the asylum seeker to a state in respect of which there is a well-founded fear of persecution or a reasonable likelihood of being tortured. Under Art. 33 of the Convention Relating to the Status of Refugees, there is a duty not to expel or return ('refouler') a refugee in any manner whatsoever to the frontiers of territories where his or her life or freedom would be threatened on account of his or her race, religion, nationality, membership of a particular social group or political opinion. The designation of safe countries to which refugees are to be sent under the Act has the consequence of avoiding the responsibility for granting asylum in a way which does not violate the principle of non-refoulement.

Removal of asylum claimants to safe third countries

Until the coming into force of the 1996 Act a person who was refused leave to enter the United Kingdom under the Immigration Act 1971 could appeal against the refusal to a special adjudicator on the ground that his or her removal in consequence of the refusal would be contrary to the United Kingdom's obligations under the Convention (1993 Act, section 8(1)).

In respect of safe third countries the Home Secretary provided the special adjudicator with a certificate specifying that the country in question could be relied upon to fulfil its Convention responsibilities. This certificate could be challenged before the special adjudicator on the ground that the third state had failed to comply with its Convention obligations in the past and therefore might well do so in the future, and the special adjudicator was empowered to require further evidence on the point from the Home Secretary. Difficult questions arose concerning the extent of disclosure required to be made by the Home Secretary concerning his or her reasons for certifying a third country to be safe. After the introduction of the Asylum and Immigration Bill, the House of Lords, in *R* v *Secretary of State for the Home Department, ex parte Abdi and Gawe* [1996] 1 WLR 298 held that the Home Secretary was not obliged to give discovery of the material on which he based his or her 'without foundation' certificate. Furthermore, a statement by the Home Secretary that, in his or her experience, a specified third country would fulfil its obligations to consider asylum, while not much, was enough to enable special adjudicators to uphold a certificate that the third country would comply with its Convention obligations.

Such certificates have been, however, challenged successfully, notably in respect of Belgium where the practice was such that an applicant who travelled on to the United Kingdom might find any later application in Belgium, after return, time-barred and where therefore it could not be said, contrary to the Home Secretary's certificate, that Belgium was a safe third country (*R* v *Special Adjudicator, ex parte Turus, The Times,* 13 May 1996).

Appeal

Under the new Act where a certificate has been issued under the above procedure the applicant may appeal to a special adjudicator on the ground that any one of the conditions mentioned in section 2(2) was not fulfilled when the certificate was issued or has ceased to be fulfilled. Unless and until the certificate is set aside on appeal he may not bring any appeal under part II of the 1971 Act or section 8 of the 1993 Act which refers to appeals to the special adjudicator on Convention grounds.

It would seem to follow that a successful challenge to the certificate could only be founded on two bases. The first is by showing that the conditions factually are not met, for example, that he is not a national or citizen of the country to which he is to be sent, or that that such a country's government does not respect the principle of 'non-refoulement'. In respect of nationality difficult issues could arise. If the claimant has renounced a given nationality but he or she is considered by the state concerned not to have done so, either because he has not taken the formal steps required by the procedure in that state, or because that state does not recognise the abandonment of citizenship, the applicant could be caught by a certificate from the foreign state confirming his or her national status.

The second ground is, presumably, to show *Wednesbury* unreasonableness, that is, that in the light of the recipient state's past practice, the Home Secretary acted unreasonably in issuing it, or is acting unreasonably in not withdrawing it.

The range of issues thus encompassed by the truncated appeal procedure is narrow and it is by no means clear what evidence a claimant will be able to rely on or what will be the standard of proof which he will be required to meet. In particular, it is not clear to what extent procedural deficiencies in the country to which the person is to be deported may be considered by the special adjudicator. In respect of the appeal against the Home Secretary's certificate, such issues would seem relevant only under ground (c) (a claim which does not show a fear of persecution by reason of the appellant's race, nationality, etc.), but that provision seems essentially to relate to state action directed towards a deliberate violation of the Convention. It is unclear whether deficiencies in a state's procedural rules which may have the effect of sending a person back to a jurisdiction where he may suffer persecution suffice to fall within the relevant condition. If a narrow approach to condition (c) is taken, it will no longer be possible to argue that the country to which the Secretary of State's certificate refers is a country which cannot be certified. Thus authorities such as *ex parte Bostam* April 1996, Hidder J, unreported (referred to in 571 HL Deb. col. 1112) will no longer be applicable. The convention issue will not be reached.

If on an appeal to which schedule 2, para. 5 of the 1993 Act (as amended) applies the special adjudicator agrees that the claim is one to which para. 4 applies (that is, that there is no fear or justified fear of persecution, or the claim is manifestly fraudulent or frivolous or vexatious) or where there is no evidence that the applicant was tortured, as noted above, there will be no right on the part of the applicant to appeal to the Immigration Appeal Tribunal under section 20(1) of the 1971 Act. This does not, however, affect the government's right to appeal from a decision of the special adjudicator in the applicant's favour.

A further restriction on appeal is provided by section 3(2): a person who is to be sent to a member state of the European Union or to a country to be designated by the Home Secretary is not entitled to bring or pursue an appeal under section 2 so long as he or she is in the United Kingdom. He or she will, therefore, have to pursue his or her appeal from the third, safe country, to which he or she has been returned or sent. An appeal has, thus, no suspensive effect, an aspect of the legislation justified by the government on the grounds that the provision only applies in relation to European Union countries and such countries as the United States of America, Canada and Switzerland which have proven safe asylum procedures, and that asylum seekers should present their claims to asylum to the first safe state at which they arrive. Where the above provision does not apply an appeal will continue to have the same suspensive effect as formerly.

The effect of these measures will be to limit drastically appeals to the special adjudicator and it will effectively insulate the government from inquiry into the rightness of its decisions. The sole protection for the asylum seeker who contends that the designated third country is not safe, either because it is likely itself to persecute the applicant on Convention grounds or return the applicant to another country in the chain which may so persecute him or her is intramural within the Home Office.

It will, of course, be difficult for individuals to mount appeals from abroad, despite the offer of an information pack to be supplied by British Embassies. Furthermore, while legal aid is in principle available for such appeals, it must be agreed in advance which, again, will presumably prove to be very difficult.

It is questionable whether the removal of the right of appeal on Convention grounds extends the ambit of judicial review. As noted above, the existence of the appeal was thought to militate against any possibility of judicial review. It may be thought, however, that Parliament, in restricting appeal, intended by implication to prevent review also. In any event, it will be difficult to show that the Home Secretary acted wholly unreasonably in reaching the decision which he did on Convention grounds, the more as the applicant will be unable to invoke any duty on the Home Office to disclose evidence.

APPEALS PROCEDURE

Procedure in respect of Asylum claims is dealt with by the Asylum Appeals (Procedure) Rules 1996 (SI 1996 No. 2070 (L.5)) which supersede all rules made earlier. This Guide reproduces the text of these rules and the commentary which follows concerns only their salient features.

Appeals to Special Adjudicator

A very short time limit applies to appeals to the Special Adjudicator from an adverse decision. The general time limit is 7 days following receipt of the decision to be appealed against. An even shorter period of 2 days applies where the following conditions apply to a claim, namely, where the applicant is refused leave to enter, where the claim is a certified claim, where the appellant is in custody in the United Kingdom, and where the decision has been served personally upon him or her.

A longer period of 28 days applies where the appeal is brought by a claimant who has been removed to a safe third country under section 3 of the 1996 Act (rule 35).

An appeal lodged out of time may, nonetheless, be treated as having been lodged within the appropriate time limit. The discretion is not, however, that of the Special Adjudicator, but that of the person to whom the Notice of Appeal is to be given. That person will either be an immigration officer (in the case of appeals under section 8(1) or (4) of the 1993 Act or the Home Secretary under section 8(2) or (3) of that Act. In either case it is for the person upon whom a notice of appeal is to be served to determine whether it is just and right to treat the notice of appeal as though it were lodged within time. No relevant considerations are indicated by the rules, and the sole recourse to any judicial authority would seem to be by way of judicial review on the ground that a failure to conclude that the time limits should be relaxed is unreasonable or at variance with the policy of the legislation, or both.

The Home Secretary is obliged to furnish certain documents to the Special Adjudicator and the appellant within 42 days of receipt of the notice of appeal. These include the notice of appeal, the original or copies of any notes of interview, and the original or copies of any other document referred to in the decision under appeal (rule 5(8)). No provision is made for the disclosure of any other document or class of documents or for the Special Adjudicator to require such disclosure.

The Notice of Appeal sets out the grounds of appeal. These may be varied by the appellant with leave of the Special Adjudicator (rule 7).

The parties to the appeal are the appellant and the Home Secretary but the United Kingdom Representative of the United Nations High Commissioner for Refugees may require as of right to be joined in such an appeal (rule 8).

In principle an appeal is to be decided within 42 days of receipt by the Special Adjudicator of the relevant documents. The Special Adjudicator may, however, extend this time limit where to do so is necessary in the interests of fairness (rule 41) in order to make a fair decision. This basic time limit applies both to appeals brought directly before the Special Adjudicator and to appeals remitted by the Immigration Appeal Tribunal to the Special Adjudicator (rule 17).

A shorter period of 10 days applies to certified claims except where the appellant appeals under section 3 of the 1996 Act from outside the United Kingdom. This, then, makes the normal period applicable where the appeal is against the designation by certificate of a country as a safe third country.

Subject to two important exceptions dealt with below, namely, the determination without hearing provisions of rule 35 and the summary decision provisions of rule 36, an appeal may not be determined without a hearing (rule 9).

The power of a Special Adjudicator to adjourn an appeal is limited to those cases where it is necessary to do so in the interests of justice. It follows that the convenience of the parties is not, as such, a relevant consideration. The Special Adjudicator is, indeed, required to pay particular heed to the need to secure the just, timely and effective conduct of the proceedings (rule 10(1) and (2)).

The Special Adjudicator may, in granting an adjournment, consider whether further directions should be given under rule 23 (rule 10(3)). He is obliged to give notice of the time and place of the adjourned hearing.

The Special Adjudicator should, in principle, announce his or her decision at the close of the hearing. He or she must, within 10 days thereof, send written notice of his or her or her determination to every party to the appeal. The period allowed is, however, one of only 5 days if the appeal relates to a certified claim. These provisions are directory rather than mandatory because the rules further provide that no notice shall be considered to be invalid by reason of any failure to comply with any time limit prescribed (rule 11).

Appeals to Immigration Appeal Tribunal

The rules further apply to appeals to the Immigration Appeal Tribunal from decisions of the Special Adjudicator.

An appeal may only be brought with the leave of the tribunal. Application for leave must be brought within 5 days of the decision in question (Tribunal Form A2 applies). This must be accompanied by the original or a copy of the determination together with all the grounds relied on. It would seem clear that a very general application may be regarded as a nullity for non-compliance with the rule. At best it would be a curable irregularity under rule 44, but whether such a defect should be considered to be a mere irregularity may well depend on the extent of non-compliance with the rule. A notice which substantially complies with the rule in respect of stating the grounds or which is is merely formally defective may be varied with leave of the tribunal (rule 13(3) read with rule 14(1)).

The tribunal must decide an application for leave within 10 days of its receipt. In principle an application for leave is dealt with on the papers unless the tribunal decides that there are special reasons which make a hearing necessary or desirable (rule 13(6)). If the tribunal fails to decide an application within the time prescribed, the application is deemed to have been granted and the appeal may proceed to a hearing on the merits (rule 13(5)).

The tribunal is obliged to send notice of its decision on leave to the parties forthwith and to furnish reasons where leave is refused (rule 13(7)).

The appellant's application for leave is treated as the Notice of Appeal and there is, therefore, no need to file any fresh document after leave has been granted. As noted, such notice may be waived with leave of the tribunal (rule 14(1)). Consistent with the emphasis on speed, the tribunal must notify the parties, within 5 days, of the date, time and place fixed for the hearing (rule 14(2)). As with the initial hearing, the local representative of the United Nations High Commissioner for Refugees may be treated as a party to the appeal (rule 15). Such a representative may only be joined when the appeal itself is under way. He may not be joined on an application for leave.

Rule 16 provides that unless the time limit is extended under rule 41 in the interests of justice, an appeal is to be decided not later than 42 days after service upon the tribunal of the appellant's notice of appeal (rule 16). It would seem that this means within 42 days of service of an application for leave since that document is treated as the notice of appeal where the application for leave is granted and since no provision is made for fresh service following a successful application. It would seem that the time limit is directory only since, unlike the deeming provision of rule 13(5), no sanction is provided for a failure by the tribunal to deal with the substantive appeal within the time limit.

As with the initial hearing, and subject to the same exceptions (rules 35 and 36), a hearing shall be held to decide an appeal. The tribunal may decide the appeal itself and will normally do so unless it considers that in the interests of justice and in order to save time and expense the case should be remitted back to a special adjudicator to be heard and determined in accordance with any directions given by the tribunal (rule 17). This power is likely, it is submitted, to be used where disputed issues of fact remain to be resolved.

Again, the power to order adjournments is subject to the same restrictions as apply in the case of the initial hearing (rule 18) and similar provision is made concerning giving notice of the result and the reasons for it (rule 19).

Appeals to the Court of Appeal or the Court of Session

Provision is made for appeals on questions of law alone (rule 20). Application for leave to appeal must be made to the tribunal within 10 days of receipt of the decision complained of (Form A3 applies). Such an application may be decided by the President or the chairman of the tribunal acting alone and will normally (that is, in the absence of special circumstances) be made without a hearing. The tribunal must notify the parties of its decision and the reasons therefor within 10 days of receipt of the application (rule 21). Once again, this time limit must be treated as directory since there is no sanction for breach of it.

General procedure

Part V of the regulations applies to the appeals noted above and to applications for bail (rule 22).

Conduct of appeals

It is for the appellate authority to regulate the procedure to be followed, subject to the rules and to the emphasis in them on the just, timely and effective disposition of appeals. The authority may give directions for the preparation and conduct of the proceedings rule 23(1) and (2)).

The authority may give directions to the parties orally or in writing. The matters in respect of which directions may be given are specified in rule 23. In brief, they include: preparation for hearing and time limits to be allowed for procedural steps; whether a matter is to be treated as a preliminary issue; whether a pre-hearing review is to be held; and whether particulars should be furnished (rule 23(4)(a)–(c)). No provision is made for discovery or disclosure and it is submitted that the matters specified in rule 23 are exhaustive, that is, the authority may make orders in respect of any or all of the enumerated matters but lacks power to go farther.

Directions may also deal with purely formal, but important, aspects of the appeal procedure. These include such matters as the preparation of bundles, the provision of skeleton arguments, lists of witnesses, and the length of time permitted for the examination of witnesses and making of submissions (rule 23(4)(d) and (e)).

The rules envisage the holding of combined hearings (under rule 34) where common questions of law or fact apply to more than one appeal and the authority may, again, give directions in respect of them (rule 23(4)(f)).

A party who fails to comply with directions may be treated as having abandoned or withdrawn the appeal. This would seem to apply to the appellant only and not to the respondent since otherwise the provision would make specific reference to the abandonment of opposition to the appeal. In the alternative the authority may simply continue with the appeal in the normal way, or determine it without a hearing under rule 35 (rule 24(1)(a)–(c)).

The authority may, however, give additional directions where it is satisfied that non-compliance with directions was attributable to circumstances beyond the control of the party in default (rule 24(2)).

Bail

An application for bail, if addressed to an immigration officer or police officer, is to be made orally. If it is addressed to an appellate authority it may be made orally or in writing (rule 25(1)).

A written application must contain certain particulars, set out in rule 25. These are straightforward. It should be noted, however, that the clear inference from the rule is that where bail has previously been denied, a renewed application is only likely to succeed where there has been a relevant change in the applicant's circumstances.

Bail may be granted but the taking of any recognizance postponed. In such a case the apppellate authority must both certify that bail has been granted and indicate what conditions are to be entered on the recognizance (rule 25).

Representation, evidence and witnesses

A party to an appeal may act in person or be represented, or may appear by counsel or solicitor appointed by a grant-assisted voluntary authority or with leave of the appellate authority by any other person appearing to the authority to be acting on behalf of the appellant. The Home Secretary or any officer of his may appear by counsel, or a solicitor, or any officer of the Home Secretary. The High Commissioner for Refugees may appoint any person to represent him or her (rule 26).

The special adjudicator and the tribunal are required to make a summary of the proceeedings (rule 43). The tribunal may receive a summary of proceedings before a Special Adjudicator as evidence (rule 27(1)).

The assumption is that such a summary shall be the primary evidence in the case. If any party to the appeal wishes to adduce further evidence he must give notice in writing indicating the nature of the evidence. The tribunal may in its discretion receive or decline to receive such evidence (rule 27(2) and (3)).

The tribunal itself may request further evidence which it must then receive.

In any event, where further evidence is received by the tribunal it may be given either orally or in writing. If the evidence is to be taken orally, it may be taken by the tribunal itself or the matter may be remitted by it to a Special Adjudicator (rule 25(3)(c)).

The appellate authorty (that is, the Special Adjudicator or the tribunal) may summon witnesses (rule 28).

The appellate authority may receive oral or written evidence and is not bound by the normal rules of admissibility. The criterion for admissibility in this context is relevance. The normal rules concerning privilege apply (rule 29).

In general every party is entitled to inspect and take copies of documentary evidence which the appellate authority takes into consideration. This is, however, subject to exception. Where it is alleged that, for example, a passport is a forgery and that disclosure to the party of the method of detection would be an inevitable concomitant of inspection or supply and would not be in the public interest, then that document shall not be supplied or made available for inspection to that party (rule 30).

A person who claims that an action should not be taken in respect of him or her because he is not a person to whom a statutory provision applies, bears the burden of proving the point. Similarly, a person who makes an assertion which he would be required to prove if he were to make it to the Home Secretary (under the Immigration Rules) bears the burden of proof on that issue (rule 31).

In general appeals are heard in public. This is subject to exceptions as provided by rule 32 and it seems unnecessary to enter into the details here.

Hearing of appeals

The appellate authority may hear an appeal in the absence of the appellant on grounds set out in rule 33 which may, compendiously, be summarised as cases where it is impossible or impracticable for him or her to attend the hearing. The appellate authority may also decide the matter in the appellant's absence where it is satisfied that the appropriate notices have been given and the appellant has not appeared and has not satisfactorily explained the reasons for his or her absence (or that of his or her representative).

Rule 34 makes provision (as already noted) for combined appeals where common issues of law or fact appear.

Determination without hearing

Rule 35 provides for cases where an appeal may be determined without a hearing. The first such case is where the Special Adjudicator, having considered written submissions, decides to allow the appeal. The second case is where the Special Adjudicator is satisfied that the appellant is outside the United Kingdom. Thirdly, such powers may be exercised where, even though the appellant is within the United Kingdom, the Special Adjudicator is satisfied that it would be impracticable to give him or her notice of the hearing. The Special Adjudicator must also be satisfied that in either case no person is authorised to represent the appellant at the hearing (rule 35(1)(a) and (b)).

Rule 35(1)(c) concerns preliminary issues and is directed towards the appellant. If the Home Secretary raises such an issue and the appellant, having been given a reasonable opportunity to do so, fails to submit a written statement relating to it, the Special Adjudicator may make a determination without hearing. Equally, he may do so if he is of the opinion that the matters put forward by the appellant in such a statement do not warrant a hearing.

Rule 35 provides two further grounds for determination without hearing. Rule 35(1)(d) refers to the case where the parties agree in writing upon the terms of a determination. Rule 35(1)(e) refers to the case where the Special Adjudicator is satisfied, having regard to the material before him or her , the nature of the issues raised, and the extent to which directions under rule 23 have been complied with, and considers that the appeal could be disposed of justly without a hearing. In this latter case written notice of the determination is to be made available for public inspection (rule 35(3)).

The same grounds apply to determination without hearing by the Immigration Appeal Tribunal (rule 35(2)).

The Special Adjudicator may decide that it is not necessary to hold a hearing where the Home Secretary has withdrawn or reversed the decision appealed against (and where notice of this has been given). The same power, to dispense with a hearing, applies where the Special Adjudicator considers that the appeal has been abandoned, or that the decision appealed against has been withdrawn (rule 35(4) and (5)).

Summary determination of appeals

Rule 36 allows an appeal to be summarily determined where the issues which it raises arise on facts in issue which have been dealt with in previous proceedings.

In such a case the appellate authority (that is, the Special Adjudicator or the tribunal) may determine the matter without a hearing provided that it first gives to the parties an opportunity to make representations to the effect that the appeal should not be determined summarily.

Notices, mixed appeals etc.

These are dealt with in rules 38 and 39 and do not appear to call for extensive comment here.

Other matters

Rule 40 applies to enable proceedings to be transferred from one Special Adjudicator to another. Rule 41, as already noted, applies to enable time limits to be extended. Rule 42 deals with when documents are deemed to have been received. Rule 43 as already noted deals with the making of a summary of proceedings. Rule 44, which is of importance in respect of whether rules are directory or mandatory, provides that any irregularity arising from a failure to comply with the rules before the appellate authority takes a decision shall not result in nullity. Instead, the appellate authority may take steps to cure the irregularity. Finally, rule 45 is a slip rule which provides for the correction of clerical errors.

IMMIGRATION OFFENCES

A principal feature of the new Act is to provide for further immigration offences. Section 4 of the 1996 Act adds a further offence to the Immigration Act 1971. Section 24(1)(aa) of the 1971 Act now provides:

> 24(1)   A person who is not a British citizen shall be guilty of an offence punishable on summary conviction with a fine of not more than level 5 on the standard scale or with imprisonment for not more than 6 months or both in any of the following cases—
>
> . . .
>
> (aa)   if, by means which include deception by him or her , he obtains or seeks to obtain leave to enter or remain in the United Kingdom

It is submitted that the offence, in context, requires that the person knowingly perpetrates a falsehood by act or omission. That is, even though deception is but one instance of forbidden means, the means concerned must, in any event, involve an element of moral turpitude on the part of the entrant. Otherwise, the specified instance, 'deception' would be cast in *mens rea* terms where the residual offence is not. Where there is deception, there seems no reason why such deception could not include a deception as to fact or as to law (particularly in respect of the law of a foreign jurisdiction) or, indeed, as to present intention. The statutory definition of 'deception' under section 15 of the Theft Act 1968 is cast in such wide terms as this. More broadly, at common law, Buckley J in *Re London and Globe Finance Corporation Limited* [1903] 1 Ch 728 at p. 732 held that to deceive is to induce a person to believe that a thing is true which is false, and in *Director of Public Prosecutions* v *Ray* [1974] AC 370 only Lord Reid (dissenting) appears to have thought that deception necessarily implies a positive act. The inquiry must surely be functional: whether what is done or omitted is intended to and does produce an erroneous belief in the sense referred to above or where the entrant is aware that such a belief may be inferred. That said, it is not inconceivable that a situation might arise in which a person seeking entry would knowingly fail to eradicate a false impression on the part of an immigration officer of which he, the entrant, was aware. In our submission this might be an instance of deception in content. It is not clear to what extent the legislation is intended to impose affirmative duties on claimants but in the context of these provisions as a whole, an affirmative duty of honesty may well be imposed. Alternatively, to rely on a known error on the part of the authorities, produced by another, might be an example of the wider means to which the section refers.

The offence does not penalise a person who travels on a false passport. It does, however, relate to the use of such a passport to gain admission or asylum. An example suggested in Committee is that of a person who presents a passport from a country with a bad human rights record in support of an asylum claim where the passport is not a passport or the principal passport to which the person is entitled (571 HL Deb col. 1928). This is, of course, a clear instance of deception.

The offence (in section 25 of the 1971 Act), of assisting persons to obtain leave by deception, has been fundamentally recast by section 5 of the 1996 Act. It now provides:

25(1) Any person knowingly concerned in making or carrying out arrangements for facilitating:

(a) the entry into the United Kingdom of anyone whom he knows or has reasonable cause for believing to be an illegal entrant;

(b) the entry into the United Kingdom of anyone whom he knows or has reasonable cause for believing to be an asylum claimant; or

(c) the obtaining by anyone of leave to remain in the United Kingdom by means which he knows or has reasonable cause for believing to include deception.

The purpose of this provision is to punish those who use and abuse the position of an asylum seeker in order to make a gain. It is not limited to remuneration but extends to any benefit which can be considered a gain. This presumably means money or money's worth.

The government's professed intention is not to penalise those who genuinely provide assistance to an asylum seeker once he is here. The section is intended to strike at those who illegally provide assistance during the asylum seeker's journey to an arrival in the United Kingdom. It is intended, *inter alia*, to strike at marriage racketeers. This emphasis is reflected in the wording of section 5(1)(c) which was specifically redrafted in order to placate the fears of those persons such as solicitors who gave *bona fide* advice to actual or potential asylum seekers.

An exemption is provided by section 5(2) (inserting a new subsection 1A into the 1971 Act ensuring that the offence of assisting an asylum claimant (section 5(1)(b)) shall not apply to anything done by a person otherwise than for gain, or in the course of his or her employment by a *bona fide* organisation whose purpose it is to assist refugees or in relation to a person who has been detained under schedule 2, para. 16 or has been granted temporary admission under para. 21.

The wording of subsection (c) is identical to that in section 4(1)(aa) and the same remarks, *mutatis mutandis*, apply. This new provision has given rise to concern by The Law Society which fears that the legislation will target those who give a proper and legitimate service to their clients as criminals (Jane Coker, 'Lawyers In The Dock', (1996) 93 LS Gazette 27). The government's response is that the provision is intended to apply to racketeers, not solicitors, and that the latter will only be liable for seeking leave to remain for a client where forged papers are used. Nonetheless, the legislation on its face exempts only non-profit-making bodies and the offence could certainly be committed by a legal adviser who is applied to for advice and assistance by an asylum claimant.

Whether the exemption is enough to meet all legitimate concerns is, perhaps, questionable. In particular, the effect of section 5(1)(b) is uncharted: in theory a solicitor or other adviser acting for reward who should know, but does not, that a person is an asylum claimant, will fall within the ambit of the offence. The government may have achieved that which was not its purpose: to criminalise what would otherwise be the lawful, if perhaps occasionally negligent, giving of legal advice.

The offence under section 25(1)(a) of the 1971 Act (as amended) attracts a measure of extraterritorial jurisdiction over the categories of persons mentioned in it. A British citizen, for example, who facilitates the entry into the United Kingdom of anyone whom he knows or has reasonable cause to believe to be an illegal entrant commits an offence even though his or her acts were done wholly outside the United Kingdom and even though the acts are preliminary in character. Liability would extend to making arrangements for the harbouring of such a person within the United Kingdom after illegal entry (see, by analogy, *R* v *Latif* [1996] 1 WLR 104).

Section 25(6) of the 1971 Act contains a forfeiture provision. The effect of the 1996 Act is to extend it to the offences of facilitating illegal entry and to facilitating the entry of an asylum seeker. An asylum claimant is simply defined as a person who intended to make a claim for asylum within the meaning of the 1993 Act.

Section 25 (as amended) is obviously broad. The phrase 'has reasonable cause for believing to be' is plainly wide. These are words of objective description (see *R* v *Emsden,* 1987, unreported and, by analogy, *R* v *Young,* [1984] 2 All ER 164) and will make liable a person who, if he did not know that the person was either an illegal entrant or an asylum seeker, should plainly have done so. The offence in its relation to asylum seekers does not require that the facilitator know or believe that the asylum seeker will endeavour to enter illegally. It is thus extremely broad, the sole defence being for those who facilitate otherwise than for gain or who act for *bona fide* organisations. This leaves within the net and liable to conviction persons (within the designated categories) who, for example, in a foreign state, advise persons for gain, even though their advice and assistance is given or done for the purpose of facilitating a proper claim. Such a person will only be protected through the discretion not to prosecute.

Section 6 of the 1996 Act applies to raise the maximum penalty under sections 24(1), 26(1) and 27 of the 1971 Act to a level 5 fine.

POWERS OF ARREST ETC.

A power of arrest without warrant is conferred by section 7(1) upon a constable or an immigration officer in respect of offences of illegal entry, obtaining leave to enter or remain by deception, or remaining beyond the time limited by leave, and of failing to observe a condition of entry (1971 Act, section 24(1)(a), (aa) and (b)). The power is predicated upon reasonable grounds for suspecting the person to have committed the offence. The constable need not be in uniform.

Section 7(2) gives power to a justice of the peace, or in Scotland a sheriff or justice of the peace, to grant a warrant authorising a constable to enter premises, by force if necessary, to search for and arrest persons suspected of having committed any of the offences specified above. The justice of the peace or the sheriff must be satisfied by written evidence on oath that there is reasonable ground for suspecting that person to be on the designated premises. The government made clear that this power can be used to force entry into churches where asylum seekers take refuge, but that such powers will be used sensitively (Standing Committee D, col. 433).

In respect of any of the offences specified, a justice, in England and Wales or Northern Ireland may, under section 8 of the Police and Criminal Evidence Act 1984, (or its Northern Irish counterpart) grant a warrant to enter and search designated premises for material which is likely to be of substantial value in the investigation of the offence and which has evidential value. For the purposes of this warrant provision, the designated immigration offences are deemed to be serious arrestable offences.

PART II

Immigrants and employment

The 1996 Act contains stringent provisions against the employment of immigrants who are not in possession of a work permit. The scheme of the Act is to penalise employers and much debate has centred around the burden thus placed on small businesses.

A person who employs a person subject to immigration control to whom the restrictions in the Act apply is guilty of an offence (section 8(1)). The offence is triable only summarily and carries a maximum penalty of a level 5 fine. No provision is made for imprisonment. This is a strict liability offence subject to an affirmative defence (the burden of which lies on the employer) that an authorised document was presented to the employer (section 8(2)). This is, however, subject to the further reservation that the defence does not apply where, in any event, the employer knew that it would be an offence to employ the individual concerned.

An employer who employs a person aged 16 or over commits an offence if either (a) the employee has not been granted leave to enter or remain in the United Kingdom, or (b) does not have a valid or subsisting leave, or is subject to a condition precluding him or her from taking up the appointment, and in either case the employee does not satisfy such conditions as may be prescribed by the Home Secretary (section 8(1)(a)–(b)).

The affirmative defence under section 8(2) requires the employer to prove both that an appropriate document was supplied to him or her and that he either retained the document or kept a copy or other record of it. The nature of the documents to be presented and the manner in which records are to be kept are both to be specified in an order of the Home Secretary.

The offence also applies to the directors, secretary, officers, and managers of a company which employs an immigrant (section 8(5) and (6)).

It seems inevitable that this provision will bear harshly on immigrants seeking employment. Even immigrants of long standing will be refused employment where they cannot prove their status. This is, however, consistent with the government's aim in passing the legislation.

PART III

Accommodation

Section 9 of the Act imposes a duty on housing authorities to secure, so far as is practicable, that housing accommodation under either Part II or Part III of the Housing Act 1985 or its Scottish or Northern Irish counterparts is not made available to any person subject to immigration control unless he falls within a class specified in an order made by the Home Secretary. Such a person will also be excluded from accommodation or assistance under the homelessness part and shall be disregarded in determining, for the purpose of the homelessness part, whether another person is homeless or threatened with homelessness, or has a priority need for accommodation. It may parenthetically be noted that this policy has largely been frustrated by the courts. In *R v Hammersmith and Fulham LBC ex p. M, The Times*, 10 October 1996, the High Court held that a destitute asylum seeker who had no money and who lacked the means to support himself could be said to be in need of care and attention within the meaning of section 21(5) of the National

Assistance Act 1948 so as to impose a duty upon a local authority to provide him with accommodation. It seems likely that this will frustrate the purpose of the Act.

In respect of section 9, however, those classes of persons to whom housing may be allocated are specified in the Housing Accommodation and Homelessness (Persons subject to Immigration Control) Order 1996 (SI 1996 No. 1982). In brief the following are the qualifying classes:

Class A – a person recorded by the Home Secretary as a refugee within Art. 1 of the Status of Refugees Convention of 1951.

Class B – a person who has been given exceptional leave to remain where such leave is not subject to any condition requiring him or her to maintain himself and his or her dependants without recourse to public funds:

Class C – a person who has current leave to enter or remain in the United Kingdom which is not subject to any limitation or condition.

Class D – an overseas student in a case where a housing authority lets accomodation to a specified educational institution for use as student accommodation and where it would otherwise be difficult to let such accommodation.

Class E (to which section 9(2) refers) – a person who makes a claim for asylum (which is not recorded as having been determined or abandoned) where the claim is recorded as made on his or her arrival (other than on his or her re-entry) in the United Kingdom from outside the common travel area, or a person who makes such a claim within 3 months from the day on which the Home Secretary makes a declaration to the effect that the country of which he is a national is subject to such a fundamental change in circumstances that he would not normally order the return of a person to that country.

Class F – a person (other than an asylum claimant falling within class E) who made a claim for asylum before 4 February 1996 and who at that date was entitled to housing benefit, provided that his or her claim is not recorded as having been abandoned or decided, or where there was at that date a timely appeal pending in respect of that claim, and in either of the two cases above the Home Secretary has not recorded that such appeal has been abandoned or determined.

It may further be noted that by virtue of paragraphs 2 and 3 of the Order, an overseas student, in order to qualify, must be studying full time which requires attendance at a specified institution of higher education for at least 15 hours per week for organised day-time study.

Those persons falling outside the classes are regarded as illegal entrants and overstayers.

The effect of this provision is to place the housing authority under a positive duty not to allocate housing to such persons even on an interim basis, and this duty will be enforceable financially against the authority. It follows that the normal statutory criteria followed in allocating housing (as to which see Housing Act 1985, sections 22 and 59) will not apply. Such persons will fall outside the safety net of the welfare state.

It should be noted that this measure will have a further impact upon housing associations. Local authorities have nomination rights to such schemes for people who are on the local authorities' housing waiting list. Such rights will not be exercisable in favour of the prohibited class noted above and a measure of private housing will thus also be denied them.

Asylum seekers who are allowed to remain become refugees and are not caught by this provision.

Section 10 provides that no immigrant within the meaning of the Asylum and Immigration Act 1996 shall be entitled to child benefit for any week unless he satisfies conditions. The effect of this (which amends the Social Security Contributions and Benefits Act 1992 by inserting a new section 146A) is that illegal immigrants and overstayers who are excluded from other benefits will also be excluded from child benefit. In effect child benefit will be restricted, in respect of a family, only where *both* partners are immigrants and have a restriction on their right of residence.

PART IV

Social security

Section 11 provides that Regulations may be made which will exclude any person who has made a claim for asylum after entry from a wide range of benefits. These are: income support, housing benefit and council tax benefit under the Social Security Contributions and Benefits Act 1992 and its Northern Irish counterpart, and jobseeker's allowance.

Regulations may provide that such a claimant may be entitled to benefit if he is subsequently recorded by the Secretary of State as a refugee within the meaning of the Convention. The details of the extent of benefit entitlement will be settled by regulations which, at the time of writing, are not available.

Even before the passing of the Act substantial changes were made to entitlement to various benefits. These are contained in The Social Security (Persons From Abroad) Miscellaneous Amendments Regulations (SI 1996, No. 30) as amended by schedule 1 to the Asylum and Immigration Act 1996. This was to meet the point that the Regulations were in part held *ultra vires* of the 1993 Act in *R v Secretary of State for Social Security, ex parte Joint Council for the Welfare of Immigrants, The Times*, 27 June 1996.

The Regulations affect entitlement to the following benefits:

Attendance Allowance
Council Tax Benefit
Disability Living Allowance
Disability Working Allowance
Family Credit
Housing Benefit

Invalid Care Allowance
Income Support
Payments on Account
Severe Disablement Allowance

In relation to those denied benefit in respect of income support, housing benefit and council tax benefit, the regulations are to have effect as if they had been made and had come into force on the day on which the Asylum and Immigration Act 1996 is passed (schedule 1, paras. 2–4). Any person who is excluded from benefit *prima facie*, and who is not entitled to benefit under the regulations or under regulations to be made by virtue of section 11(2) of the 1996 Act shall not be entitled to the benefit for any period beginning on the day after the Act is passed, and shall not be entitled to any benefit for the period beginning on or after 5 February 1996 except on a claim made before the day on which the Act is passed, or any application made before that day for the review of a decision. This preserves claims and applications for judicial review which were already in the pipeline. Similar provision is made in respect of Northern Ireland (schedule 1, part II).

The scheme for entitlement or disentitlement in relation to asylum seekers (the coverage of the regulations is rather broader) requires that the person be recorded as a refugee within the relevant international instruments, or is a person who comes to Britain as his or her first country of refuge and claims asylum on arrival on Convention grounds. Provision is also made for a person who becomes an asylum seeker while (lawfully) in Great Britain, as for example where conditions have changed in his or her own country so that, on political grounds, it is unsafe for him or her to return.

The conditions which apply in this latter case are onerous. The Secretary of State must make a declaration to the effect that the country of which he is a national is subject to such a fundamental change in circumstances that he would not normally order the return of a person to that country. The individual must, within 3 months from the date upon which such a declaration was made, submit a claim to the Home Secretary under the Status of Refugees Convention. His claim for asylum under the Convention must be duly recorded by the Home Secretary.

It will be observed that the Home Secretary is under no duty to make such a declaration. No doubt an individual could seek to promote such a declaration (for example through his or her member of Parliament) but the Home Secretary is under no duty to act upon it and, indeed, such an inquiry might well provoke an examination of the individual's case in a manner that could well be detrimental to him or her.

PART V

The schedules

Schedule 2 to the 1996 Act amends the 1971 and 1993 Acts in significant respects. These are dealt with only to the extent that their purport may require elucidation.

Paragraph 1(1) amends the general provisions for regulation and control by extending the conditions which may be imposed on persons given limited leave to enter or remain. Whereas provisions enabling an immigration officer to impose conditions on reporting to the police and restrictions on employment formerly existed, section 3 of the 1971 Act now permits a condition to be imposed upon a person given limited leave to enter or remain that he or she maintain and accommodate himself or herself and his or her dependants without recourse to public funds.

This provision also amends section 3(5) of the 1971 Act, adding to those who may be deported a person who has obtained leave to remain by deception.

Paragraph 2 of schedule 1 was said to be animated solely by a desire to promote sexual equality. The effect of it is that for the purposes of deportation, a husband of a woman who is to be deported may now himself be deported. Thus, where a man is to be deported his wife and children under the age of 18 years may also be deported, and where a woman is to be deported her husband and children under the age of 18 years may also be deported (assuming, of course, that the spouse has not an independent right to remain (section 3(5) of the 1971 Act as amended).

Paragraph 3 in respect of appeals against conditions adds subsection (22A) to the 1971 Act, the effect of which is that a person may not appeal against a condition requiring him or her to support himself or his dependants, or against a refusal to vary his leave by revoking such a condition (schedule 2, para. 3(1)(a)–(b)). Paragraph 3 further amends section 14(2B) of the 1971 Act. The effect of the amendment is that a person cannot appeal under section 41(1) of the 1971 Act against any refusal to vary his leave if the refusal is on the ground that a relevant document which is required by the Immigration Rules has not been issued, and it adds to 'relevant document' under section 14(2B) approvals to work issued after entry (work permits being already covered).

Paragraph 4 is an interpretation provision, which defines 'entrant' and 'illegal entrant'. The latter provision is now cast in terms which include a person who enters or seeks to enter by means which include deception by another person. There is nothing in this definition to suggest that the category only applies to those who are aware that a deception is being used: that is, the status does not depend on any complicity on the part of the entrant. A further effect of para. 4 is that an appeal is treated as pending until it is finally determined or withdrawn or is abandoned by reason of the appellant leaving the United Kingdom.

The effect of para. 5(1) is that a person being examined by an immigration officer may be required to declare whether he is carrying or conveying or has carried or conveyed documents of any relevant description specified by the immigration officer (amending schedule 2, para. 4 of the 1971 Act).

Paragraph 5(2)(a) permits search of a person who is required to declare whether he is or has carried or conveyed documents of a class falling within amended schedule 2, para. 4 of the 1971 Act. Paragraph 5(2)(b) is wider. It permits search of the person, and any baggage or vehicle belonging to him or her or under his or her control and any ship or aircraft or vehicle in which he arrived in the United Kingdom.

Paragraph 6 amends schedule 2, para. 9 of the 1971 Act. This now empowers an immigration officer, in the case of an illegal entrant, to give directions to the captain or owner of a ship or aircraft on which he has arrived to remove him or her, and any leave to enter the United Kingdom which has been obtained by deception is to be disregarded for these purposes. The effect of the amendment is very wide. What matters is that the leave have been obtained by deception. It seems not to be required that the entrant be party to any dishonesty or knowingly have deceived. Equally, the obligations imposed upon the carrier do not depend upon it or its servants or agents having been aware of any flaw in any documentation offered by or on behalf of the entrant. This is certainly Draconian.

Paragraph 6 amends para. 9 of schedule 2 to the 1971 Act which deals with the removal of illegal entrants. The effect is that directions for removal of an illegal entrant may be given by an immigration officer (as before), but by the new subparagraph (c) any leave to enter which has been obtained by deception is to be disregarded.

Paragraph 10 amends the provisions of para. 21 of schedule 2 of the 1971 Act. Its effect is that a person who is subject to a restriction as to reporting to an immigration officer with a view to the conclusion of his or her examination and who fails to comply with it may be dealt with as though his or her examination was concluded and he need not be notified within 24 hours that he is refused leave.

Paragraph 11 materially affects bail provisions relating to persons subject to detention. A person who is detained under para. 11(1) of schedule 2 to the 1971 Act pending examination, or who is detained under schedule 2, para. (2) pending the giving of directions may be released on bail. This power is exercisable by an immigration officer not below the rank of chief immigration officer, or an adjudicator. Release may be recognizance (or in Scotland bail bond) conditional for his or her appearance before the immigration officer at a specified time or place.

The power to release on bail may not, however, be exercised unless 7 days have elapsed since his or her arrival in the United Kingdom. Bail may also be made subject to such conditions as the adjudicator considers are likely to ensure the person's presence at the required time and place.

Finally, para. 12 inserts a new para. 34 to schedule 2 of the 1971 Act. The bail provisions which apply to persons detained for examination also apply to persons who are detained pending removal. It may be surmised that bail will be granted in few such cases.

Schedule 3 effects significant amendments to the 1993 Act. Section 7 of that Act concerns curtailment of leave to enter or remain.

Schedule 3, para. 1 adds a new subsection (1A) to section 7 of the 1993 Act. The effect is that where the Home Secretary by notice curtails the duration of leave to enter or remain (where the person claims that it would be contrary to the United Kingdom's obligation under the Convention to require him or her to leave after the time limited by the leave and the Home Secretary has requested this) he may also, by notice, curtail the duration of leave of that person's dependant or dependants. The remaining provisions extend the ban on appeal and enable the making of a deportation order against such a person.

Schedule 3, para. (2) materially restricts appeals to a Special Adjudicator by inserting subsection (1A) into section 8 of the 1993 Act. At present a person against whom the Home Secretary has decided to make or has refused to revoke a deportation order may appeal on one or other ground but not both. The effect (upon section 8 of the 1993 Act) is that a person cannot appeal against revocation if he has a right of appeal against the making of a deportation order, even though he failed to exercise it.

Paragraph 3 inserts a (new) section 9A into the 1993 Act. This deals with bail pending appeal from an Immigration Appeal Tribunal. Section 9A gives power to release an appellant on bail. This applies both to pending appeals and to applications for leave to appeal. A chief immigration officer, or a police officer not below the rank of inspector or an adjudicator may exercise the power. Release may be ordered on recognizance (or in Scotland, bail bond). The Immigration Appeal Tribunal may also release a person on bail. If the appeal or application for leave is by the Home Secretary, or the appellant has been granted leave to appeal, and has given notice of appeal, the tribunal shall grant bail at the appellant's request.

Asylum and Immigration Act 1996

CHAPTER 49

ARRANGEMENT OF SECTIONS

Asylum claims

SCHEDULES

Asylum and Immigration Act 1996

1996 CHAPTER 49

An Act to amend and supplement the Immigration Act 1971 and the Asylum and Immigration Appeals Act 1993; to make further provision with respect to persons subject to immigration control and the employment of such persons; and for connected purposes. [24th July 1996]

BE IT ENACTED by the Queen's most Excellent Majesty, by and with the advice and consent of the Lords Spiritual and Temporal, and Commons, in this present Parliament assembled, and by the authority of the same, as follows:—

Asylum claims

1. Extension of special appeals procedures

For paragraph 5 of Schedule 2 to the Asylum and Immigration Appeals Act 1993 ('the 1993 Act') there shall be substituted the following paragraph—

'5.—(1) This paragraph applies to an appeal by a person on any of the grounds mentioned in subsections (1) to (4) of section 8 of this Act if the Secretary of State has certified that, in his opinion, the person's claim on the ground that it would be contrary to the United Kingdom's obligations under the Convention for him to be removed from, or be required to leave, the United Kingdom is one to which—

    (a) sub-paragraph (2), (3) or (4) below applies; and

    (b) sub-paragraph (5) below does not apply.

(2) This sub-paragraph applies to a claim if the country or territory to which the appellant is to be sent is designated in an order made by the Secretary of State by statutory instrument as a country or territory in which it appears to him that there is in general no serious risk of persecution.

(3) This sub-paragraph applies to a claim if, on his arrival in the United Kingdom, the appellant was required by an immigration officer to produce a valid passport and either—

    (a) he failed to produce a passport without giving a reasonable explanation for his failure to do so; or

(b) he produced a passport which was not in fact valid and failed to inform the officer of that fact.

(4) This sub-paragraph applies to a claim if—

(a) it does not show a fear of persecution by reason of the appellant's race, religion, nationality, membership of a particular social group, or political opinion;

(b) it shows a fear of such persecution, but the fear is manifestly unfounded or the circumstances which gave rise to the fear no longer subsist;

(c) it is made at any time after the appellant—

(i) has been refused leave to enter under the 1971 Act,

(ii) has been recommended for deportation by a court empowered by that Act to do so,

(iii) has been notified of the Secretary of State's decision to make a deportation order against him by virtue of section 3(5) of that Act, or

(iv) has been notified of his liability to removal under paragraph 9 of Schedule 2 to that Act;

(d) it is manifestly fraudulent, or any of the evidence adduced in its support is manifestly false; or

(e) it is frivolous or vexatious.

(5) This sub-paragraph applies to a claim if the evidence adduced in its support establishes a reasonable likelihood that the appellant has been tortured in the country or territory to which he is to be sent.

(6) Rules of procedure under section 22 of the 1971 Act may make special provision in relation to appeals to which this paragraph applies.

(7) If on an appeal to which this paragraph applies the special adjudicator agrees that the claim is one to which—

(a) sub-paragraph (2), (3) or (4) above applies; and

(b) sub-paragraph (5) above does not apply,

section 20(1) of that Act shall not confer on the appellant any right to appeal to the Immigration Appeal Tribunal.

(8) The first order under this paragraph shall not be made unless a draft of the order has been laid before and approved by a resolution of each House of Parliament.

(9) A statutory instrument containing a subsequent order under this paragraph shall be subject to annulment in pursuance of a resolution of either House of Parliament.

(10) In this paragraph—

"immigration officer" means an immigration officer appointed for the purposes of the 1971 Act;

"passport", in relation to an appellant, means a passport with photograph or some other document satisfactorily establishing his identity and nationality or citizenship.'

2. Removal etc. of asylum claimants to safe third countries

(1)   Nothing in section 6 of the 1993 Act (protection of claimants from deportation etc.) shall prevent a person who has made a claim for asylum being removed from the United Kingdom if—

(a)   the Secretary of State has certified that, in his opinion, the conditions mentioned in subsection (2) below are fulfilled;

(b)   the certificate has not been set aside on an appeal under section 3 below; and

(c)   except in the case of a person who is to be sent to a country or territory to which subsection (3) below applies, the time for giving notice of such an appeal has expired and no such appeal is pending.

(2)   The conditions are—

(a)   that the person is not a national or citizen of the country or territory to which he is to be sent;

(b)   that his life and liberty would not be threatened in that country or territory by reason of his race, religion, nationality, membership of a particular social group, or political opinion; and :

(c)   that the government of that country or territory would not send him to another country or territory otherwise than in accordance with the Convention.

(3)   This subsection applies to any country or territory which is or forms part of a member State, or is designated for the purposes of this subsection in an order made by the Secretary of State by statutory instrument.

(4)   The first order under this section shall not be made unless a draft of the order has been laid before and approved by a resolution of each House of Parliament.

(5)   A statutory instrument containing a subsequent order under this section shall be subject to annulment in pursuance of a resolution of either House of Parliament.

(6)   For the purposes of this section, an appeal under section 3 below is pending during the period beginning when notice of appeal is duly given and ending when the appeal is finally determined or withdrawn.

(7)   In this section 'claim for asylum' and 'the Convention' have the same meanings as in the 1993 Act.

3. Appeals against certificates under section 2

(1)   Where a certificate has been issued under section 2(1) above in respect of any person—

(a)   that person may appeal against the certificate to a special adjudicator on the ground that any of the conditions mentioned in section 2(2) above was not fulfilled when the certificate was issued, or has since ceased to be fulfilled; but

(b)   unless and until the certificate is set aside on such an appeal, he shall not be entitled to bring or pursue any appeal under—

(i)   Part II of the 1971 Act (appeals: general); or

(ii)   section 8 of the 1993 Act (appeals to special adjudicator on Convention grounds),

as respects matters arising before his removal from the United Kingdom.

(2)   A person who has been, or is to be, sent to a country or territory to which section 2(3) above applies shall not be entitled to bring or pursue an appeal under this section so long as he is in the United Kingdom.

(3)   The Lord Chancellor shall designate such number of the adjudicators appointed for the purposes of Part II of the 1971 Act as he thinks necessary to act as special adjudicators for the purposes of this section and may from time to time vary that number and the persons who are so designated.

(4)   Subject to subsection (5) below, the following provisions of the 1971 Act, namely—

(a)   section 18 (notice of decisions appealable under that Part and statement of appeal rights etc.);

(b)   section 19 (determination of appeals under that Part by adjudicators);

(c)   section 21 (references of cases by Secretary of State for further consideration);

(d)   section 22(1) to (4), (6) and (7) (rules of procedure for appeals);

(e)   section 23 (grants to voluntary organisations helping persons with rights of appeal); and

(f)   Schedule 5 (provisions about adjudicators and Immigration Appeal Tribunal),

shall have effect as if this section were contained in Part II of that Act.

(5)   Rules of procedure under section 22 of the 1971 Act—

(a)   may make special provision in relation to appeals under this section; and

(b)   may make different provision in relation to appeals by persons who have been, or are to be, sent to countries or territories of different descriptions;

and so much of paragraph 5 of Schedule 5 to that Act as relates to the allocation of duties among the adjudicators shall have effect subject to subsection (3) above.

(6)   Paragraph 29 of Schedule 2 to the 1971 Act (grant of bail pending appeal) shall have effect as if the references to appeals under sections 13(1), 15(1)(a) and 16 of that Act included references to appeals under this section.

Immigration offences

4. Obtaining leave by deception

In subsection (1) of section 24 of the 1971 Act (illegal entry and similar offences), after paragraph (a) there shall be inserted the following paragraph—

'(aa)   if, by means which include deception by him, he obtains or seeks to obtain leave to enter or remain in the United Kingdom;'.

5. Assisting asylum claimants, and persons seeking to obtain leave by deception

(1)   In subsection (1) of section 25 of the 1971 Act (assisting illegal entry, and habouring), for the words from 'the entry' to 'illegal entrant' there shall be substituted the following paragraphs—

'(a)   the entry into the United Kingdom of anyone whom he knows or has reasonable cause for believing to be an illegal entrant;

(b)   the entry into the United Kingdom of anyone whom he knows or has reasonable cause for believing to be an asylum claimant; or

(c)   the obtaining by anyone of leave to remain in the United Kingdom by means which he knows or has reasonable cause for believing to include deception,'.

(2)   After that subsection there shall be inserted the following subsection—

'(1A)   Nothing in subsection (1)(b) above shall apply to anything which is done—

(a)   by a person otherwise than for gain, or in the course of his employment by a bona fide organisation whose purpose it is to assist refugees; or

(b)   in relation to a person who has been detained under paragraph 16 of Schedule 2 to this Act, or has been granted temporary admission under paragraph 21 of that Schedule;

and in that provision ''asylum claimant'' means a person who intends to make a claim for asylum (within the meaning of the Asylum and Immigration Appeals Act 1993).'

(3)   In subsection (5) of that section, for the words 'Subsection (1)' there shall be substituted the words 'Subsection (1)(a)'.

(4)   In subsection (6) of that section, for the words 'subsection (1)' there shall be substituted the words 'subsection (1)(a) or (b)'.

6. Increased penalties
In the following provisions, namely—

(a)   subsection (1) of section 24 of the 1971 Act (illegal entry and similar offences);

(b)   subsection (1) of section 26 (general offences in connection with administration of Act); and

(c)   section 27 (offences by persons connected with ships or aircraft or with ports), for the words 'level 4' there shall be substituted the words 'level 5'.

7. Power of arrest and search warrants
(1)   A constable or immigration officer may arrest without warrant anyone whom he has reasonable grounds for suspecting to have committed an offence to which this section applies.

(2)   If—

(a)   a justice of the peace is by written information on oath satisfied that there is reasonable ground for suspecting that a person who is liable to be arrested under subsection (1) above is to be found on any premises; or

(b)   in Scotland, a sheriff, or a justice of the peace, having jurisdiction in the place where the premises are situated is by evidence on oath so satisfied, he may grant a warrant authorising any constable to enter, if need be by force, the premises named in the warrant for the purposes of searching for and arresting that person.

(3)   The following provisions, namely—

(a)   section 8 of the Police and Criminal Evidence Act 1984 (power of justice to authorise entry and search of premises); and

(b)   Article 10 of the Police and Criminal Evidence (Northern Ireland) Order 1989 (corresponding provision for Northern Ireland),
shall have effect as if the reference in subsection (1) of that section or, as the case may be, paragraph (1) of that Article to a serious arrestable offence included a reference to an offence to which this section applies.

(4)   This section applies to the following offences under section 24(1) of the 1971 Act, namely—

(a)   an offence under paragraph (a) (illegal entry);

(b)   an offence under paragraph (aa) (obtaining leave to enter or remain by deception); and

(c)   an offence under paragraph (b) (remaining beyond time limited by leave or failing to observe condition of leave).

(5)   In this section 'immigration officer' has the same meaning as in the 1971 Act.

Persons subject to immigration control

8.   Restrictions on employment

(1)   Subject to subsection (2) below, if any person ('the employer') employs a person subject to immigration control ('the employee') who has attained the age of 16, the employer shall be guilty of an offence if—

(a)   the employee has not been granted leave to enter or remain in the United Kingdom; or

(b)   the employee's leave is not valid and subsisting, or is subject to a condition precluding him from taking up the employment,
and (in either case) the employee does not satisfy such conditions as may be specified in an order made by the Secretary of State.

(2)   Subject to subsection (3) below, in proceedings under this section, it shall be a defence to prove that—

(a)   before the employment began, there was produced to the employer a document which appeared to him to relate to the employee and to be of a description specified in an order made by the Secretary of State; and

(b)   either the document was retained by the employer, or a copy or other record of it was made by the employer in a manner specified in the order in relation to documents of that description.

(3)   The defence afforded by subsection (2) above shall not be available in any case where the employer knew that his employment of the employee would constitute an offence under this section.

(4)   A person guilty of an offence under this section shall be liable on summary conviction to a fine not exceeding level 5 on the standard scale.

(5)   Where an offence under this section committed by a body corporate is proved to have been committed with the consent or connivance of, or to be attributable to any neglect on the part of—

(a)   any director, manager, secretary or other similar officer of the body corporate; or

(b)   any person who was purporting to act in any such capacity,

he as well as the body corporate shall be guilty of the offence and shall be liable to be proceeded against and punished accordingly.

(6)   Where the affairs of a body corporate are managed by its members, subsection (5) above shall apply in relation to the acts and defaults of a member in connection with his functions of management as if he were a director of the body corporate.

(7)   An order under this section shall be made by statutory instrument which shall be subject to annulment in pursuance of a resolution of either House of Parliament.

(8)   In this section—

'contract of employment' means a contract of service or apprenticeship, whether express or implied, and (if it is express) whether it is oral or in writing;
'employ' means employ under a contract of employment and 'employment' shall be construed accordingly.

9.   Entitlement to housing accommodation and assistance

(1)   Each housing authority shall secure that, so far as practicable, no tenancy of, or licence to occupy, housing accommodation provided under the accommodation Part is granted to a person subject to immigration control unless he is of a class specified in an order made by the Secretary of State.

(2)   A person subject to immigration control—

(a)   shall not be eligible for accommodation or assistance under the homelessness Part; and

(b)   shall be disregarded in determining, for the purposes of that Part, whether another person—

(i)   is homeless or is threatened with homelessness; or

(ii)   has a priority need for accommodation,

unless he is of a class specified in an order made by the Secretary of State.

(3)   An order under this section—

(a)   may make different provision for different circumstances or for accommodation or assistance of different descriptions; and

(b)   shall be made by statutory instrument which shall be subject to annulment in pursuance of a resolution of either House of Parliament.

(4)   In this section—

'the accommodation Part' and 'the homelessness Part' mean respectively—

(a)   in relation to England and Wales, Parts II and III of the Housing Act 1985;

(b)   in relation to Scotland, Parts I and II of the Housing (Scotland) Act 1987;

(c)   in relation to Northern Ireland, Part II of the Housing (Northern Ireland) Order 1981 and Part II of the Housing (Northern Ireland) Order 1988;
'housing authority' means—

(a)   in relation to England and Wales, a local housing authority within the meaning of the Housing Act 1985;

(b)   in relation to Scotland, a local authority within the meaning of the Housing (Scotland) Act 1987;

(c)   in relation to Northern Ireland, the Northern Ireland Housing Executive;

'licence to occupy', in relation to Scotland, means a permission or right to occupy;

'tenancy', in relation to England and Wales, has the same meaning as it has in the Housing Act 1985.

10.   Entitlement to child benefit

(1)   The provision set out in subsection (2) below shall be inserted—

(a)   after section 146 of the Social Security Contributions and Benefits Act 1992, as section 146A of that Act; and

(b)   after section 142 of the Social Security Contributions and Benefits (Northern Ireland) Act 1992, as section 142A of that Act.

(2)   The provision is as follows—

'**Persons subject to immigration control**. No person subject to immigration control within the meaning of the Asylum and Immigration Act 1996 shall be entitled to child benefit for any week unless he satisfies prescribed conditions.'

11.   Saving for social security regulations

(1)   Notwithstanding any enactment or rule of law, regulations may exclude any person who has made a claim for asylum from entitlement to any of the following benefits, namely—

(a)   income support, housing benefit and council tax benefit under the Social Security Contributions and Benefits Act 1992;

(b)   income support and housing benefit under the Social Security Contributions and Benefits (Northern Ireland) Act 1992; and

(c)   jobseeker's allowance under the Jobseekers Act 1995 or the Jobseekers (Northern Ireland) Order 1995.

(2)   Regulations may provide that, where such a person who is so excluded is subsequently recorded by the Secretary of State as a refugee within the meaning of the Convention—

(a)   that person may, within a prescribed period, claim the whole or any prescribed proportion of any income support, housing benefit or council tax benefit to which he would have been entitled had he been recorded as a refugee immediately after he made the claim for asylum; and

(b)   where he makes such a claim as is mentioned in paragraph (a) above in respect of housing benefit or council tax benefit having resided in the areas of two or more local authorities in Great Britain, the claim shall be investigated and determined, and any benefit awarded shall be paid or allowed, by such one of those authorities as may be prescribed.

(3)   Regulations making such provision as is mentioned in subsection (2)(b) above may require the other authorities there mentioned to supply the prescribed authority with such information as it may reasonably require in connection with the exercise of its functions under the regulations.

(4)   Schedule 1 to this Act—

(a)   Part I of which modifies the Social Security (Persons from Abroad) Miscellaneous Amendments Regulations 1996; and

(b)   Part II of which modifies the Social Security (Persons from Abroad) (Miscellaneous Amendments) Regulations (Northern Ireland) 1996,
shall have effect.

(5)   The Jobseeker's Allowance (Amendment) Regulations 1996 shall have effect as if they had been made on the day on which this Act is passed.

(6)   In this section—
'claim for asylum' and 'the Convention' have the same meanings as in the 1993 Act;
'prescribed' means prescribed by regulations;
'regulations'—

(a)   in relation to income support, housing benefit or council tax benefit under the Social Security Contributions and Benefits Act 1992, means regulations under that Act or the Social Security Administration Act 1992;

(b)   in relation to income support or housing benefit under the Social Security Contributions and Benefits (Northern Ireland) Act 1992, means regulations under that Act or the Social Security Administration (Northern Ireland) Act 1992;

(c)   in relation to jobseeker's allowance under the Jobseekers Act 1995, means regulations under that Act or the Social Security Administration Act 1992;

(d)   in relation to jobseeker's allowance under the Jobseekers (Northern Ireland) Order 1995, means regulations under that Order or the Social Security Administration (Northern Ireland) Act 1992.

Miscellaneous and supplemental

12.   Other amendments and repeals

(1)   Schedule 2 to this Act (which contains amendments of the 1971 Act and a related amendment of the Immigration Act 1988) shall have effect.

(2)   Schedule 3 to this Act (which contains amendments of the 1993 Act) shall have effect.

(3)   The enactments specified in Schedule 4 to this Act are hereby repealed to the extent specified in the third column of that Schedule.

13.   Short title interpretation, commencement and extent

(1)   This Act may be cited as the Asylum and Immigration Act 1996.

(2)   In this Act—
'the 1971 Act' means the Immigration Act 1971;

'the 1993 Act' means the Asylum and Immigration Appeals Act 1993;

'person subject to immigration control' means a person who under the 1971 Act requires leave to enter or remain in the United Kingdom (whether or not such leave has been given).

(3) This Act, except section 11 and Schedule 1, shall come into force on such day as the Secretary of State may by order made by statutory instrument appoint, and different days may be appointed for different purposes.

(4) An order under subsection (3) above may make such transitional and supplemental provision as the Secretary of State thinks necessary or expedient.

(5) Her Majesty may by Order in Council direct that any of the provisions of this Act shall extend, with such modifications as appear to Her Majesty to be appropriate, to any of the Channel Islands or the Isle of Man.

(6) This Act extends to Northern Ireland.

SCHEDULES

Section 11(4)   SCHEDULE 1   MODIFICATIONS OF SOCIAL SECURITY REGULATIONS

PART I   SOCIAL SECURITY (PERSONS FROM ABROAD) MISCELLANEOUS AMENDMENTS REGULATIONS 1996

Preliminary

1. In this Part of this Schedule—

(a) 'the 1996 Regulations' means the Social Security (Persons from Abroad) Miscellaneous Amendments Regulations 1996; and

(b) expressions which are used in the 1996 Regulations have the same meanings as in those Regulations.

Income support

2. In regulation 8 of the 1996 Regulations (amendment of the Income Support Regulations)—

(a) paragraph (2) so far as relating to the sub-paragraph added to regulation 21(3) of the Income Support Regulations as sub-paragraph (j); and

(b) paragraph (3)(c) and (d),

shall have effect as if the 1996 Regulations had been made, and had come into force, on the day on which this Act is passed.

Housing benefit

3. In regulation 7 of the 1996 Regulations (amendment of regulation 7A of the Housing Benefit Regulations)—

(a) paragraph (a) so far as relating to the sub-paragraph added to regulation 7A(4) of the Housing Benefit Regulations as sub-paragraph (g);

(b) paragraph (b) so far as relating to sub-paragraphs (a) and (b) of the paragraph substituted for regulation 7A(5) of those Regulations; and

    (c)   paragraph (c),
shall have effect as if the 1996 Regulations had been made, and had come into force, on the day on which this Act is passed.

Council tax benefit

4. In regulation 3 of the 1996 Regulations (amendment of regulation 4A of the Council Tax Benefit Regulations)—

    (a)   paragraph (a) so far as relating to the sub-paragraph added to regulation 4A(4) of the Council Tax Benefit Regulations as sub-paragraph (g);

    (b)   paragraph (b) so far as relating to sub-paragraphs (a) and (b) of the paragraph substituted for regulation 4A(5) of those Regulations; and

    (c)   paragraph (c),
shall have effect as if the 1996 Regulations had been made, and had come into force, on the day on which this Act is passed.

General

5. Regulation 12(1) of the 1996 Regulations (saving) shall have effect as if after the words 'shall continue to have effect' there were inserted the words '(both as regards him and as regards persons who are members of his family at the coming into force of these Regulations)'.

6.—(1) Subject to sub-paragraph (2) below, any person who is excluded from entitlement to income support, housing benefit or council tax benefit by any of the provisions which are modified by the preceding provisions of this Part of this Schedule—

    (a)   shall not be entitled to the benefit for any period beginning on or after the day on which this Act is passed; and

    (b)   shall not be entitled to the benefit for any period beginning on or after 5th February 1996 except on a claim made before the day on which this Act is passed, or an application made before that day for the review of a decision.

(2) Nothing in this paragraph shall apply in any case where a person is entitled to the benefit in question either—

    (a)   by virtue of regulation 12(1) of the 1996 Regulations (saving); or

    (b)   by virtue of regulations making such provision as is mentioned in section 11(2) of this Act.

PART II SOCIAL SECURITY (PERSONS FROM ABROAD) (MISCELLANEOUS AMENDMENTS) REGULATIONS (NORTHERN IRELAND) 1996

Preliminary

7. In this Part of this Schedule 'the 1996 Regulations' means the Social Security (Persons from Abroad) (Miscellaneous Amendments) Regulations (Northern Ireland) 1996.

Income support

8.　In regulation 4 of the 1996 Regulations (amendment of the Income Support (General) Regulations)—

(a)　paragraph (2) so far as relating to the paragraph added to regulation 21(3) of the Income Support (General) Regulations (Northern Ireland) 1987 as paragraph (j); and

(b)　paragraph (3)(b),

shall have effect as if the 1996 Regulations had been made, and had come into operation, on the day on which this Act is passed.

Housing benefit

9.　In regulation 5 of the 1996 Regulations (amendment of the Housing Benefit (General) Regulations)—

(a)　paragraph (a) so far as relating to the sub-paragraph added to regulation 7A(4) of the Housing Benefit (General) Regulations (Northern Ireland) 1987 as sub-paragraph (g);

(b)　paragraph (b) so far as relating to sub-paragraphs (a) and (b) of the paragraph substituted for regulation 7A(5) of those Regulations; and

(c)　paragraph (c),

shall have effect as if the 1996 Regulations had been made, and had come into operation, on the day on which this Act is passed.

General

10.　Regulation 11(1) of the 1996 Regulations (saving) shall have effect as if after the words 'shall have effect' there were inserted the words '(both as regards him and as regards persons who are members of his family at the coming into operation of these Regulations)'.

11.—(1)　Subject to sub-paragraph (2) below, any person who is excluded from entitlement to income support or housing benefit by any of the provisions which are modified by the preceding provisions of this Part of this Schedule—

(a)　shall not be entitled to the benefit for any period beginning on or after the day on which this Act is passed; and

(b)　shall not be entitled to the benefit for any period beginning on or after 5th February 1996 except on a claim made before the day on which this Act is passed, or an application made before that day for the review of a decision.

(2)　Nothing in this paragraph shall apply in any case where a person is entitled to the benefit in question either—

(a)　by virtue of regulation 11(1) of the 1996 Regulations (saving); or

(b)　by virtue of regulations making such provision as is mentioned in section 11(2) of this Act.

Section 50   SCHEDULE 2   AMENDMENTS OF THE 1971 ACT
AND THE IMMIGRATION ACT 1988

General provisions for regulation and control, &c.

1.—(1) In subsection (1) of section 3 of the 1971 Act (general provisions for regulation and control), for paragraph (c) there shall be substituted the following paragraph—

'(c)   if he is given limited leave to enter or remain in the United Kingdom, it may be given subject to all or any of the following conditions, namely—

(i)   a condition restricting his employment or occupation in the United Kingdom;

(ii)   a condition requiring him to maintain and accommodate himself, and any dependants of his, without recourse to public funds; and

(iii)   a condition requiring him to register with the police.'

(2) In subsection (5) (persons liable to deportation) of that section, after paragraph (a) there shall be inserted the following paragraph—

'(aa) if he has obtained leave to remain by deception; or'.

(3) In subsection (1) of section 5 of the Immigration Act 1988 (restricted right of appeal against deportation), after paragraph (a) there shall be inserted the following paragraph—

'(aa)   by virtue of section 3(5)(aa) of that Act (leave obtained by deception); or'.

Persons belonging to another's family

2.   In subsection (4) of section 5 of the 1971 Act (persons belonging to another's family), for paragraph (b) there shall be substituted the following paragraph—

'(b)   where that other person is a woman, her husband and her or his children under the age of eighteen;'.

Appeals against conditions

3.—(1) After subsection (2) of section 14 of the 1971 Act (appeals against conditions), there shall be inserted the following subsection—

'(2ZA)   A person shall not be entitled to appeal under subsection (1) above against—

(a)   a variation of his leave which adds such a condition as is mentioned in section 3(1)(c)(ii) above; or

(b)   a refusal to vary his leave by revoking such a condition.'

(2) In subsection (2B) of that section, for paragraph (c) there shall be substituted the following paragraph—

'(c)   work permits, or equivalent documents issued after entry.'

Interpretation

4.—(1) In subsection (1) of section 33 of the 1971 Act (interpretation), for the definitions of 'entrant' and 'illegal entrant' there shall be substituted the following definitions—

' "entrant" means a person entering or seeking to enter the United Kingdom and "illegal entrant" means a person—

(a)   unlawfully entering or seeking to enter in breach of a deportation order or of the immigration laws, or

(b)   entering or seeking to enter by means which include deception by another person,

and includes also a person who has entered as mentioned in paragraph (a) or (b) above;'.

(2)   In subsection (4) of that section, after the words 'determined or withdrawn', in the first place where they occur, there shall be inserted the words 'or is abandoned by reason of the appellant leaving the United Kingdom'.

Information and documents

5.—(1)   In sub-paragraph (2)(b) of paragraph 4 of Schedule 2 to the 1971 Act (information and documents), after the words 'is carrying or conveying', in the first place where they occur, there shall be inserted the words ', or has carried or conveyed,'.

(2)   In sub-paragraph (3) of that paragraph—

(a)   after the words 'is carrying or conveying' there shall be inserted the words ', or has carried or conveyed,';

(b)   for the words from 'he and any' to 'control' there shall be substituted the following paragraphs—

'(a)   he and any baggage or vehicle belonging to him or under his control; and

(b)   any ship, aircraft or vehicle in which he arrived in the United Kingdom,'; and

(c)   after the words 'is doing' there shall be inserted the words 'or, as the case may be, has done'.

Removal of illegal entrants

6.   Paragraph 9 of Schedule 2 to the 1971 Act (removal of illegal entrants) shall be renumbered as sub-paragraph (1) of that paragraph; and after that provision as so renumbered there shall be inserted the following sub-paragraph—

'(2)   Any leave to enter the United Kingdom which is obtained by deception shall be disregarded for the purposes of this paragraph.'

Arrest of persons liable to detention

7.   In sub-paragraph (2)(b) of paragraph 17 of Schedule 2 to the 1971 Act (arrest of persons liable to detention), the words 'magistrate or' shall cease to have effect.

Recovery of expenses incurred in detaining persons refused leave to enter

8.   In sub-paragraph (1) of paragraph 19 of Schedule 2 to the 1971 Act (recovery of expenses incurred in detaining persons refused leave to enter), for the

words 'at any time' there shall be substituted the words 'for any period (not exceeding 14 days)'.

Recovery of expenses incurred in detaining illegal entrants

9.—(1) In sub-paragraph (1) of paragraph 20 of Schedule 2 to the 1971 Act (recovery of expenses incurred in detaining illegal entrants), for the words 'at any time' there shall be substituted the words 'for any period (not exceeding 14 days)'.

(2) After that sub-paragraph there shall be inserted the following sub-paragraph—

'(1A) Sub-paragraph (1) above shall not apply to expenses in respect of an illegal entrant if he obtained leave to enter by deception and the leave has not been cancelled under paragraph 6(2) above.'.

Temporary admission of persons liable to detention

10. After sub-paragraph (2) of paragraph 21 of Schedule 2 to the 1971 Act (temporary admission of persons liable to detention) there shall be inserted the following sub-paragraphs—

'(3) Sub-paragraph (4) below applies where a person who is at large in the United Kingdom by virtue of this paragraph is subject to a restriction as to reporting to an immigration officer with a view to the conclusion of his examination under paragraph 2 above.

(4) If the person fails at any time to comply with that restriction—

(a) an immigration officer may direct that the person's examination under paragraph 2 above shall be treated as concluded at that time; but

(b) nothing in paragraph 6 above shall require the notice giving or refusing him leave to enter the United Kingdom to be given within twenty-four hours after that time.'

Temporary release of persons liable to detention

11.—(1) For sub-paragraph (1) of paragraph 22 of Schedule 2 to the 1971 Act (temporary release of persons liable to detention) there shall be substituted the following sub-paragraphs—

'(1) The following, namely—

(a) a person detained under paragraph 16(1) above pending examination; and

(b) a person detained under paragraph 16(2) above pending the giving of directions,

may be released on bail in accordance with this paragraph.

(1A) An immigration officer not below the rank of chief immigration officer or an adjudicator may release a person so detained on his entering into a recognizance or, in Scotland, bail bond conditioned for his appearance before an immigration officer at a time and place named in the recognizance or bail bond or at such other time and place as may in the meantime be notified to him in writing by an immigration officer.

(1B)   Sub-paragraph (1)(a) above shall not apply unless seven days have elapsed since the date of the person's arrival in the United Kingdom.'

(2)   In sub-paragraph (2) of that paragraph—

(a)   for the word 'adjudicator', in the first place where it occurs, there shall be substituted the words 'immigration officer or adjudicator'; and

(b)   for the word 'adjudicator', in the second place where it occurs, there shall be substituted the words 'officer or adjudicator'.

(3)   In sub-paragraph (3) of that paragraph—

(a)   for the word 'adjudicator', in the first place where it occurs, there shall be substituted the words 'immigration officer or adjudicator'; and

(b)   for the word 'adjudicator', in the second and third places where it occurs, there shall be substituted the words 'officer or adjudicator'.

'Grant of bail pending removal

12.   After paragraph 33 of Schedule 2 to the 1971 Act there shall be inserted the following paragraph—

'Grant of bail pending removal

34.—(1)   Paragraph 22 above shall apply in relation to a person—

(a)   directions for whose removal from the United Kingdom are for the time being in force; and

(b)   who is for the time being detained under Part I of this Schedule, as it applies in relation to a person detained under paragraph 16(1) above pending examination or detained under paragraph 16(2) above pending the giving of directions.

(2)   Paragraphs 23 to 25 above shall apply as if any reference to paragraph 22 above included a reference to that paragraph as it applies by virtue of this paragraph.'

Supplementary provisions as to deportation

13.   In paragraph 2(5) of Schedule 3 to the 1971 Act (supplementary provisions as to deportation), after the words 'the police' there shall be inserted the words 'or an immigration officer'.

Section 12(2)   SCHEDULE 3
                    AMENDMENTS OF THE 1993 ACT

Curtailment of leave to enter or remain

1.—(1)   After subsection (1) of section 7 of the 1993 Act (curtailment of leave to enter or remain) there shall be inserted the following subsection—

'(1A)   Where the Secretary of State by notice under subsection (1) above curtails the duration of any person's leave to enter or remain in the United Kingdom, he may also by notice in writing given to any dependant of that person curtail to the same extent the duration of that dependant's leave so to enter or remain.'

(2)   In subsections (2), (3) and (4) of that section, for the words 'subsection (1) above' there shall be substituted the words 'subsection (1) or (1A) above'.

Appeals to special adjudicator

2.—(1)   In subsection (3) of section 8 of the 1993 Act (appeals to special adjudicator), the words from 'but a person' to the end shall cease to have effect.

(2)   After that subsection there shall be inserted the following subsection—

'(3A)   A person may not appeal under paragraph (b) of subsection (3) above if he has had the right to appeal under paragraph (a) of that subsection, whether or not he has exercised it.'

Bail pending appeal from Immigration Appeal Tribunal

3.   After section 9 of the 1993 Act there shall be inserted the following section—

'9A.   Bail pending appeal from Immigration Appeal Tribunal

(1)   Where a person ("an appellant")—

(a)   has an appeal under Part II of the 1971 Act which is pending by reason of an appeal, or an application for leave to appeal, under section 9 above; and

(b)   is for the time being detained under Part I of Schedule 2 to that Act (general provisions as to control on entry etc.),

he may be released on bail in accordance with this section.

(2)   An immigration officer not below the rank of chief immigration officer, a police officer not below the rank of inspector or an adjudicator may release an appellant on his entering into a recognizance or, in Scotland, bail bond conditioned for his appearance before the appropriate appeal court at a time and place named in the recognizance or bail bond.

(3)   The Immigration Appeal Tribunal may release an appellant on his entering into a recognizance or, in Scotland, bail bond conditioned for his appearance before the appropriate appeal court at a time and place named in the recognizance or bail bond; and where—

(a)   the appeal, or the application for leave to appeal, under section 9 above is by the Secretary of State; or

(b)   the appellant has been granted leave to appeal under that section, and has duly given notice of appeal,

the Tribunal shall, if the appellant so requests, exercise its powers under this subsection.

(4)   Sub-paragraphs (5) and (6) of paragraph 29 (grant of bail pending appeal) of Schedule 2 to the 1971 Act shall apply for the purposes of this section as they apply for the purposes of that paragraph.

(5)   Paragraphs 30 to 33 of that Schedule shall apply as if—

(a)   any reference to paragraph 29 included a reference to this section;

(b) the reference in paragraph 30(2) to paragraph 29(3) or (4) included a reference to subsection (3) above; and

(c) any reference in paragraphs 31 to 33 to the Immigration Appeal Tribunal included a reference to the appropriate appeal court.

(6) In this section 'the appropriate appeal court' has the same meaning as in section 9 above.'

Security of tenure

4. In paragraph 6(1) of Schedule 1 to the 1993 Act (security of tenure)—

(a) after the words 'Part III of the Act of 1985' there shall be inserted the words 'or Part II of the Act of 1987'; and

(b) after the words ' the Housing Act 1988' there shall be inserted the words 'or the Housing (Scotland) Act 1988'.

Appeals to special adjudicator: supplementary

5. In paragraph 4(2) of Schedule 2 to the 1993 Act (appeals to special adjudicator: supplementary), for the word 'and' immediately following paragraph (f) there shall be substituted the following paragraph—

'(ff) section 33(4) (duration of appeals); and'.

Section 12(3)   SCHEDULE 4
                                  REPEALS

Chapter	Short title	Extent of repeal
1971 71 c. 77.	Immigration Act 1971.	In Schedule 2, in paragraph 17(2)(b), the words 'magistrate or'.
1993 c. 23.	Asylum and Immigration Appeals Act 1993.	In section 8(3), the words from 'but a person' to the end.

Asylum and Immigration Appeals Act 1993

(Consolidated form as amended by the Asylum and Immigration Act 1996)

CHAPTER 23

ARRANGEMENT OF SECTIONS

Introductory

Asylum and Immigration Appeals Act 1993

(Consolidated with amendments)
1993 CHAPTER 23

An Act to make provision about persons who claim asylum in the United Kingdom and their dependants; to amend the law with respect to certain rights of appeal under the Immigration Act 1971; and to extend the provisions of the Immigration (Carriers' Liability) Act 1987 to transit passengers. [1st July 1993]

BE IT ENACTED by the Queen's most Excellent Majesty, by and with the advice and consent of the Lords Spiritual and Temporal, and Commons, in this present Parliament assembled, and by the authority of the same, as follows:

Introductory

1. Interpretation
In this Act—
    'the 1971 Act' means the Immigration Act 1971;
    'claim for asylum' means a claim made by a person (whether before or after the coming into force of this section) that it would be contrary to the United Kingdom's obligations under the Convention for him to be removed from, or required to leave, the United Kingdom; and
    'the Convention' means the Convention relating to the Status of Refugees done at Geneva on 28th July 1951 and the Protocol to that Convention.

2. Primacy of Convention
Nothing in the immigration rules (within the meaning of the 1971 Act) shall lay down any practice which would be contrary to the Convention.

Treatment of persons who claim asylum

3. Fingerprinting
    (1)   Where a person ('the claimant') has made a claim for asylum, an immigration officer, constable, prison officer or officer of the Secretary of State authorised for the purposed of this section may—

(a)   take such steps as may be reasonably necessary for taking the claimant's fingerprints; or

(b)   by notice in writing require the claimant to attend at a place specified in the notice in the order that such steps may be taken.

(2)   The powers conferred by subsection (1) above may be exercised not only in relation to the claimant but also in relation to any dependant of his; but in the exercise of the power conferred by paragraph (a) of that subsection, fingerprints shall not be taken from a person under the age of sixteen' ('the child') except in the presence of a person of full age who is—

(a)   the child's parent or guardian; or

(b)   a person who for the time being takes responsibility for the child and is not an immigration officer, constable, prison officer or officer of the Secretary of State.

(3)   Where the claimant's claim for asylum has been finally determined or abandoned—

(a)   the powers conferred by subsection (1) above shall not be exercisable in relation to him or any dependant of his; and

(b)   any requirement imposed on him or any dependant of his by a notice under subsection (1)(b) above shall no longer have effect.

(4)   A notice given to any person under paragraph (b) of subsection (1) above—

(a)   shall give him a period of at least seven days within which he is to attend as mentioned in that paragraph; and

(b)   may require him so to attend at a specified time of day or between specified times of day.

(5)   Any immigration officer or constable may arrest without warrant a person who has failed to comply with a requirement imposed on him by a notice under subsection (1)(b) above (unless the requirement no longer has effect) and, where a person is arrested under this subsection,—

(a)   he may be removed to a place where his fingerprints may conveniently be taken, and

(b)   (whether or not he is so removed) there may be taken such steps as may be reasonably necessary for taking his fingerprints before he is released.

(6)   Fingerprints of a person which are taken by virtue of this section must be destroyed not later than the earlier of—

(a)   the end of the period of one month beginning with any day on which he is given indefinite leave under the 1971 Act to enter or remain in the United Kingdom; and

(b)   the end of the period of ten years beginning with the day on which the fingerprints are taken.

(7)   Where fingerprints taken by virtue of this section are destroyed—

(a)   any copies of the fingerprints shall also be destroyed; and

(b)   if there are any computer data relating to the fingerprints, the Secretary of State shall, as soon as it is practicable to do so, make it impossible for access to be gained to the data.

(8) If—

    (a)   subsection (7)(b) above falls to be complied with, and

    (b)   the person to whose fingerprints the data relate for a certificate that it has been complied with,

such a certificate shall be issued to him by the Secretary of State not later than the end of the period of three months beginning with the day on which he asks for it.

(9) In this section—

    (a)   'immigration officer' means an immigration officer appointed for the purposes of the 1971 Act; and

    (b)   'dependant', in relation to the claimant, means a person—

        (i)   who is his spouse or a child of his under the age of eighteen; and

        (ii)   who has neither a right to abode in the United Kingdom nor indefinite leave under the 1971 Act to enter or remain in the United Kingdom.

(10) Nothing in this section shall be taken to limit the power conferred by paragraph 18(2) of Schedule 2 to the 1971 Act.

4. Housing of Asylum seekers and their dependants

(1) If a person ('the applicant') makes an application under the homelessness legislation for accommodation or assistance in obtaining accommodation and the housing authority who are dealing with his case are satisfied—

    (a)   that he is an asylum-seeker or the dependant of an asylum seeker, and

    (b)   that he has or has available for his occupation any accommodation, however temporary, which it would be reasonable for him to occupy,

nothing in the homelessness legislation shall require the housing authority to secure that accommodation is made available for his occupation.

(2) In determining for the purposes of subsection (1)(b) above whether it would be reasonable for the applicant to occupy accommodation, regard may be had to the general circumstances prevailing in relation to housing in the district of the housing authority who are dealing with the applicant's case.

(3) Where, on an application made as mentioned in subsection (1) above, the housing authority are satisfied that the applicant is an asylum seeker or the dependant of an asylum-seeker, but are not satisfied as mentioned in paragraph (b) of that subsection, then, subject to subsection (4) below,

    (a)   any duty under the homelessness legislation to secure that accommodation is made available for the applicant's occupation shall not continue after he ceases to be an asylum seeker or a dependant of an asylum seeker; and

    (b)   accordingly, so long as the applicant remains an asylum-seeker or the dependant of an asylum-seeker, any need of his for accommodation shall be regarded as temporary only.

(4) If, immediately before he ceases to be an asylum seeker or the dependant of an asylum-seeker, the applicant is occupying accommodation (whether temporary or not) made available in pursuance of the homelessness legislation, that legislation shall apply as if, at that time—

    (a)   he were not occupying that accommodation and

(b)   he had made an application under that legislation for accommodation or assistance in obtaining accommodation to the housing authority who secured that accommodation was made available.

(5)   Schedule 1 to this Act (which makes supplementary provision with respect to housing of asylum-seekers and their dependants) shall have effect.

5.   Housing: interpretative provisions

(1)   The provisions of this section have effect for the purposes of section 4 above and Schedule 1 to this Act; and that section and Schedule are in the following provisions of this section referred to as 'the housing provisions'.

(2)   For the purposes of the housing provisions a person who makes a claim for asylum—

(a)   becomes an asylum-seeker at the time when his claim is recorded by the Secretary of State as having been made; and

(b)   ceases to be an asylum-seeker at the time when his claim is recorded by the Secretary of State as having been finally determined or abandoned.

(3)   For the purposes of the housing provisions, a person—

(a)   becomes a dependant of an asylum-seeker at the time when he is recorded by the Secretary of State as being a dependant of the asylum seeker; and

(b)   ceases to be dependant of an asylum-seeker at the time when the person whose dependant he is ceases to be an asylum-seeker or, if it is earlier, at the time when he is recorded by the Secretary of State as ceasing to be a dependant of the asylum seeker.

(4)   References in subsections (2) and (3) above to a time when an event occurs include references to a time before as well as after the passing of this Act.

(5)   In relation to an asylum-seeker, 'dependant' means a person—

(a)   who is his spouse or a child of his under the age of eighteen; and

(b)   who has neither a right of abode in the United Kingdom nor indefinite leave under the 1971 Act to enter or remain in the United Kingdom.

(6)   Except in their application to Northern Ireland, in the housing provisions—

(a)   'the homelessness legislation' means, in relation to England and Wales, Part III of the housing Act 1985 and, in relation to Scotland, Part II of the Housing (Scotland) Act 1987;

(b)   'housing authority' means—

(i)   in relation to England and Wales, any authority which is a local housing authority for the purposes of Part III of the Housing Act 1985; and

(ii)   in relation to Scotland, any authority which is a local authority for the purposes of Part II of the Housing (Scotland) Act 1987;

and references to a housing authority who are dealing with an applicant's case shall be construed as references to the authority to whom the application is made or (as the case may be) the authority who under the homelessness legislation are the notified authority in relation to the applicant.

(7)   In the application of the housing provisions to Northern Ireland—

(a) 'the homelessness legislation' means Part II of the Housing (Northern Ireland) Order 1988;

(b) 'housing authority' means the Northern Ireland Housing Executive and references to a housing authority who are dealing with an applicant's case shall be construed as references to that Executive; and

(c) references to the district of a housing authority shall be construed as references to Northern Ireland.

(8) For the purposes of the housing provisions accommodation shall be regarded as available for the applicant's occupation only if it is available for occupation both by him and by any other person who might reasonably be expected to reside with him and references to securing accommodation for his occupation shall be construed accordingly.

6. Protection of claimants from deportation etc.

During the period beginning when a person makes a claim for asylum and ending when the Secretary of State gives him notice of the decision on the claim; he may not be removed from; or required to leave, the United Kingdom.

7. Curtailment of leave to enter or remain

(1) Where—

(a) a person who has limited leave under the 1971 Act to enter or remain in the United Kingdom claims that it would be contrary to the United Kingdom's obligations under the Convention for him to be required to leave the United Kingdom after the time limited by the leave, and

(b) the Secretary of State has considered the claim and given to the person notice in writing of his rejection of it,

the Secretary of State may by notice in writing, given to the person concurrently with the notice under paragraph (b) above, curtail the duration of the leave.

(1A) Where the Secretary of State by notice under subsection (1) above curtails the duration of any person's leave to enter or remain in the United Kingdom, he may also by notice in writing given to any dependant of that person curtail to the same extent the duration of that dependant's leave so to enter or remain.'

(2) No appeal may be brought under section 14 of the 1971 Act or section 8(2) below against the curtailment of leave under subsection (1) or (1A) above.

(3) The power conferred by subsection (1) or (1A) above is without prejudice to sections 3(3) and 4 of the 1971 Act and the immigration rules (within the meaning of the Act).

(4) Where—

(a) the duration of a person's leave under the 1971 Act to enter or remain in the United Kingdom has been curtailed under [subsection (1) or (1A) above], and

(b) the Secretary of State has decided to make a deportation order against him by virtue of section 3(5) of that Act,

he may be detained under the authority of the Secretary of State pending the making of deportation order; and the references to sub-paragraph (2) of paragraph

2 of Schedule 3 to that Act in sub-paragraphs (3), (4) and (6) of that paragraph (provisions about detention under sub-paragraph (2)) shall include references to this subsection.

Rights of Appeal

8. Appeals to special adjudicator

(1)   A person who is refused leave to enter the United Kingdom under the 1971 Act may appeal against the refusal to a special adjudicator on the ground that his removal in consequence of the refusal would be contrary to the United Kingdom's obligations under the Convention.

(2)   A person who has limited leave under the 1971 Act to enter or remain in the United Kingdom may appeal to a special adjudicator against any variation of, or refusal to vary, the leave on the ground that it would be contrary to the United Kingdom's obligations under the Convention for him to be required to leave the United Kingdom after the time limited by the leave.

(3)   Where the Secretary of State—

(a)   has decided to make a deportation order against a person by virtue of section 3(5) of the 1971 Act, or

(b)   has refused to revoke a deportation order made against a person by virtue of section 3(5) or (6) of that Act,

the person may appeal to a special adjudicator against the decision or refusal on the ground that his removal in pursuance of the order would be contrary to the United Kingdom's obligations under the Convention.

[(3A) A person may not appeal under paragraph (b) of subsection (3) above if he has had the right to appeal under paragraph (a) of that subsection, whether or not he has exercised it.]

(4)   Where directions are given as mentioned in section 16(1)(a) or (b) of the 1971 Act for a person's removal from the United Kingdom, the person may appeal to a special adjudicator against the directions on the ground that his removal in pursuance of the directions would be contrary to the United Kingdom's obligations under the Convention.

(5)   The Lord Chancellor shall designate such number of the adjudicators appointed for the purposes of Part II of the 1971 Act as he thinks necessary to act as special adjudicators for the purposes of this section and may from time to time vary that number and the persons who are so designated.

(6)   Schedule 2 to this Act (which makes supplementary provision about appeals under this section) shall have effect; and the preceding provisions of this section shall have effect subject to that Schedule.

9. Appeals from Immigration Appeal Tribunal

(1)   Where the Immigration Appeal Tribunal has made a final determination of an appeal brought under Part II of the 1971 Act (including that Part as it applies by virtue of Schedule 2 to this Act) any party to the appeal may bring a further appeal to the appropriate appeal court on any question of law material to that determination.

(2) An appeal under this section may be brought only with the leave of the Immigration Appeal Tribunal or, if such leave is refused, with the leave of the appropriate appeal court.

(3) In this section 'the appropriate appeal court' means—

(a) if the appeal is from the determination of an adjudicator or special adjudicator and that determination was made in Scotland, the Court of Session: and

(b) in any other case, the Court of Appeal.

(4) Rules of procedure under section 22 of the 1971 Act may include provision regulating, and prescribing the procedure to be followed on, applications to the Immigration Appeal Tribunal for leave to appeal under this section.

(5) In section 33(4) of the 1971 Act—

(a) for the words 'in the case of an appeal to an adjudicator, the' there shall be substituted 'an' and

(b) after the words 'section 20' there shall be inserted 'or section 9 of the Asylum and Immigration Appeals Act 1993'.

[9A. Bail pending appeal from Immigration Appeal Tribunal

(1) Where a person ('an appellant')

(a) has an appeal under Part II of the 1971 Act which is pending by reason of an appeal, or an application for leave to appeal, under section 9 above; and

(b) is for the time being detained under Part I of Schedule 2 to that Act (general provisions as to control on entry etc).

he may be released on bail in accordance with this section.

(2) An immigration officer not below the rank of chief immigration officer, a police officer not below the rank of inspector or an adjudicator may release an appellant on his entering into a recognizance or in Scotland bail bond conditioned for his appearance before the appropriate appeal court at a time and place named in the recognizance or bail bond.

(3) The Immigration Appeal Tribunal may release an appellant on his entering into a recognizance or, in Scotland, bail bond conditioned for his appearance before the appropriate appeal court at a time and placed named in the recognizance or bail bond; and where—

(a) the appeal, or the application for leave to appeal, under section 9 above is by the Secretary of State; or

(b) the appellant has been granted leave to appeal under that section, and has duly given notice of appeal,

the Tribunal shall, if the appellant so requests, exercise its powers under this subsection.

(4) Sub-paragraphs (5) and (6) of paragraph 29 (grant of bail pending appeal) of Schedule 2 to the 1971 Act shall apply for the purposes of this section as they apply for the purposes of that paragraph.

(5) Paragraphs 30 to 33 of that Schedule shall apply as if—

(a) any reference to paragraph 29 included a reference to this section;

(b) the reference in paragraph 30(2) to paragraph 29(3) or (4) included a reference to subsection (3) above; and

(c) any reference in paragraphs 31 to 33 to the Immigration Appeal Tribunal included a reference to the appropriate appeal court.

(6) In this section 'the appropriate appeal court' has the same meaning as in section 9 above.']

10. Visitors, short-term and prospective students and their dependants

In section 13 of the 1971 Act (appeals against exclusion from United Kingdom), after subsection (3) there shall be inserted—

(3A) A person who seeks to enter the United Kingdom

(a) as a visitor, or

(b) in order to follow a course of study of not more than six months duration for which he has been accepted, or

(c) with the intention of studying but without having been accepted for any course of study, or

(d) as a dependant of a person within paragraph (a), (b) or (c) above,

shall not be entitled to appeal against a refusal of an entry clearance and shall not be entitled to appeal against a refusal of leave to enter unless he held a current entry clearance at the time of the refusal.

(3AA) The Secretary of State shall appoint a person, not being an officer of his, to monitor, in such manner as the Secretary of State may determine, refusals of entry clearances in cases where there is, by virtue of subsection (3A) above, no right of appeal; and the person so appointed shall make an annual report on the discharge of his functions to the Secretary of State who shall lay a copy of it before each House of Parliament.

(3AB) The Secretary of State may pay to a person appointed under Subsection (3AA) above such fees and allowances as he may with the approval of the Treasury determine.

11. Refusals which are mandatory under immigration rules

(1) In section 13 of the 1971 Act, after subsection (3AB) (which is inserted by section 10 above) there shall be inserted

(3B) A person shall not be entitled to appeal against a refusal of an entry clearance if the refusal is on the ground that—

(a) he or any person whose dependant he is does not hold a relevant document which is required by the immigration rules; or

(b) he or any person whose dependant he is does not satisfy a requirement of the immigration rules as to age or nationality or citizenship; or

(c) he or any person whose dependant he is seeks entry for a period exceeding that permitted by the immigration rules;

and a person shall not be entitled to appeal against a refusal of leave to enter if the refusal is one any of those grounds.

(3C) For the purposes of subsection (3B)(a) above, the following are 'relevant documents'—

(a) entry clearances;

(b) passports or other identity documents; and

(c) work permits.

(2) In section 14 of the 1971 Act (appeals against refusals to vary leave to enter or remain), after subsection (2) there shall be inserted—

(2A) A person shall not be entitled to appeal under subsection (1) above against any refusal to vary his leave if the refusal is on the ground that—

(a) a relevant document which is required by the immigration rules has not been issued; or

(b) the person or a person whose dependant he is does not satisfy a requirement of the immigration rules as to age or nationality or citizenship; or

(c) the variation would result in the duration of the person's leave exceeding what is permitted by the immigration rules; or

(d) any fee required by or under any enactment has not been paid.

(2B) For the purposes of subsection (2A)(a) above, the following are relevant documents—

(a) entry clearances;

(b) passports or other identity documents; and

(c) work permits.

Visa for transit passengers

12. Carrier's liability for transit passengers

(1) The Immigration (Carriers' Liability) Act 1987 shall be amended as follows.

(2) In subsection (1)(b) of section 1 (liability of carrier of person who requires a visa for entry but fails to produce one) for the words, 'a visa valid for that purpose', there shall be substituted the words or by virtue of section 1A below requires a visa for passing through the United Kingdom, a visa valid for the purpose of entering or (as the case may be) passing through the United Kingdom.

(3) After that section there shall be inserted—

'1A. Visas for transit passengers

(1) The Secretary of State may by order require persons of any descriptions specified in the order who on arrival in the United Kingdom pass through to another country or territory without entering the United Kingdom to hold a visa for that purpose.

(2) An order under this section—

(a) may specify a description of persons by reference to nationality, citizenship, origin or other connection with any particular country or territory, but not by reference to race, colour or religion;

(b) shall not provide for the requirement imposed by the order to apply to any person who under the Immigration Act 1971 has the right of abode in the United Kingdom and may provide for any category of persons of a description specified in the order to be exempted from the requirement imposed by the order and—

(c)   may make provision about the method of application for visas required by the order.

(3)   An order under this section shall be made by statutory instrument which shall be made by statutory instrument which shall be subject to annulment in pursuance of a resolution of either House of Parliament.'

Supplementary

13.   Financial provision

(1)   There shall be paid out of money provided by Parliament—

(a)   any expenditure incurred by the Secretary of State under this Act; and

(b)   any increase attributable to this Act in the sums payable out of such money under any other enactment.

(2)   Any sums received by the Secretary of State by virtue of this Act shall be paid into the Consolidated Fund.

14.   Commencement

(1)   Sections 4 to 11 above (and section 1 above so far as it relates to those sections) shall not come into force until such day as the Secretary of State may by order appoint, and different days may be appointed for different provisions or for different purposes.

(2)   An order under subsection (1) above—

(a)   shall be made by statutory instrument; and

(b)   may contain such transitional and supplemental provisions as the Secretary of State thinks necessary or expedient.

(3)   Without prejudice to the generality of subsections (1) and (2) above, with respect to any provision of section 4 above an order under subsection (1) above may appoint different days in relation to different descriptions of asylum-seekers and dependants of asylum-seekers; and any such descriptions may be framed by reference to nationality, citizenship, origin or other connection with any particular country or territory, but not by reference to race, colour or religion.

15.   Extent

(1)   Her Majesty may by Order in Council direct that any of the provisions of this Act shall extend, with such modifications as appear to Her Majesty to be appropriate, to any of the Channel Islands or the Isle of Man.

(2)   This Act extends to Northern Ireland.

16.   Short title

This Act may be cited as the Asylum and Immigration Appeals Act 1993.

SCHEDULES

Section 4(5)   SCHEDULE 1

HOUSING OF ASYLUM-SEEKERS AND THEIR DEPENDANTS:
SUPPLEMENTARY

Qualifying persons

1.   In this Schedule the expression 'qualifying person' means an asylum-seeker or
a dependant of an asylum-seeker.

Inquiries about applicants

2.   If a housing authority to whom an application is made have reason to believe that
the applicant is a qualifying person, they shall include in the inquires that they are
required to make under section 62 of the Housing Act 1985, section 28 of the Housing
(Scotland) Act 1987 or, as the case may be, Article 7 of the Housing (Northern
Ireland) order 1988 such inquiries as are necessary to satisfy them as to whether—

   (a)   he is a qualifying person; and

   (b)   if so, whether any duty is owed to him to secure that accommodation is
made available for his occupation.

Notification of decision and reasons

3.—(1)   Subject to sub-paragraph (2) below, if a housing authority who are dealing
with an applicant's case are satisfied that he is a qualifying person they shall notify him

   (a)   that they are so satisfied;

   (b)   that they are or, as the case may be, are not satisfied that a duty is owed
to him to secure that accommodation is made available for his occupation;

   (c)   if they are the authority to whom the application is made, whether they
have notified or propose to notify another housing authority under section 67 of
the Act 1985 or, as the case may be, section 33 of the Act of 1987 (referral of
application on grounds of local connection) as modified by paragraph 4 below;
and they shall at the same time notify him of their reasons.

   (2)   In its application to Northern Ireland, sub-paragraph (1) above shall have
effect as if paragraph (c) were omitted.

   (3)   The notice required to be given to the applicant under sub-paragraph (1)
above shall be given in writing and shall, if not received by him, be treated as
having been given to him only if it is made available at the authority's office for
a reasonable period for collection by him or on his behalf.

   (4)   Where notice is given under sub-paragraph (1) above, no notice need be
given under section 64 of the Act of 1985, section 30 of the Act of 1987 or, as the
case may be, Article 9 of the Order of 1988 (notification of decision and reasons).

Referral of application to another housing authority

4.—(1)   If a housing authority to whom an application is made are satisfied that
the applicant is a qualifying person and that a duty to secure that accommodation

is made available for his occupation is owed to him, the homelessness legislation shall have effect as if in section 67 of the Act of 1985 or, as the case may be, section 33 of the Act of 1987 for paragraph (a) of subsection (1) there were substituted—

(a)   are satisfied that an applicant is a qualifying person and that a duty to secure that accommodation is made available for his occupation is owed to him.

(2)   Sub-paragraph (1) above does not apply in relation to Northern Ireland.

Offences

5.   Section 74 of the Act of 1985, section 40 of the Act of 1987 or, as the case may be, Article 17 of the Order of 1988 applies to statements made or information withheld with intent to induce an authority to believe that a person is or is not an asylum-seeker or a dependant of an asylum-seeker as it applies to statements made or information withheld with the intent mentioned in subsection (1) of section 74, section 40 or, as the case may be, Article 17.

Security of tenure

6.—(1)   A tenancy granted in pursuance of any duty under Part III of the Act of 1985 or part II of the Act of 1987 to a person who is a qualifying person cannot be—

(a)   a tenancy which is a secure tenancy for the purposes of that Act, or

(b)   a tenancy which is an assured tenancy for the purposes of the Housing Act 1988 or the Housing (Scotland) Act 1988

before the expiry of the period of twelve months beginning with the date on which the landlord is supplied with written information given by the Secretary of State under paragraph 7 below that the person has ceased to be a qualifying person, unless before the expiry of that period the landlord notifies that person that the tenancy is to be regarded as a secure tenancy or, as the case may be, an assured tenancy.

(2)   A tenancy granted in pursuance of any duty under Part II of the Order of 1988 to a person who is a qualifying person cannot be a tenancy which is a secure tenancy for the purposes of Part II of the Housing (Northern Ireland) Order 1983 before the expiry of the period of twelve months beginning with the date on which the landlord is supplied with written information given by the Secretary of State under paragraph 7 below that the person has ceased to be a qualifying person, unless before the expiry of that period the landlord notifies that person that the tenancy is to be regarded as a secure tenancy.

Information

7.—(1)   The Secretary of State shall, if requested to do so by a housing authority who are dealing with an applicant's case, inform the authority whether the applicant has become a qualifying person.

(2)   Where information which the Secretary of State is required to give to a housing authority under sub-paragraph (1) above is given otherwise than in writing, he shall confirm it in writing if a written request is made to him by the authority.

(3) If the Secretary of State informs an authority that an applicant has become a qualifying person, he shall, when the applicant ceases to be a qualifying person, inform the authority and the applicant in writing of that event and of the date on which it occurred.

Existing Applicants

8.—(1) Nothing in section 4 or section 5 of this Act or this Schedule shall affect—

(a) the right of any person to occupy (or to have made available for his occupation) accommodation which, immediately before the day on which section 4 comes into force, is required to be made available for his occupation in pursuance of the homelessness legislation; or

(b) any application made to a housing authority which immediately before that day is a pending application.

(2) For the purposes of sub-paragraph (1) above an application shall be regarded as pending if it is an application in respect of which the authority have not completed the inquiries that they are required to make under section 62 of the Housing Act 1985, section 28 of the Housing (Scotland) Act 1987 or, as the case may be, Article 7 of the Housing (Northern Ireland) Order 1988.

Isles of Scilly

9.—(1) The provisions of sections 4 and 5 of this Act and this Schedule shall apply to the Isles of Scilly subject to such exceptions, adaptations and modifications as the Secretary of State may by order direct.

(2) An order under sub-paragraph (1) above shall be made by statutory instrument which shall be subject to annulment in pursuance of a resolution of either House of Parliament.

Section 8(6)   SCHEDULE 2

APPEALS TO SPECIAL ADJUDICATOR: SUPPLEMENTARY

New appeal rights to replace rights under the 1971 Act

1. No appeal may be brought under Part II of the 1971 Act on any of the grounds mentioned in subsections (1) to (4) of section 8 of this Act.

Scope of New Rights of Appeal

2. A person may not bring an appeal on any grounds mentioned in subsections (1) to (4) of section 8 of this Act unless, before the time of refusal, variation, decision or directions (as the case may be), he has made a claim for asylum.

Other grounds for appeal

3. Where an appeal is brought by a person on any of the grounds mentioned in subsections (1) to (4) of section 8 of this Act, the special adjudicator shall in the same proceedings deal with—

(a)   any appeal against the refusal, variation, decision or directions (as the case may be) which the person is entitled to bring under Part II of the 1971 Act on any other ground on which he seeks to rely; and

(b)   any appeal brought by the person under that Part of that Act against any other decision or action.

Application of procedures in the 1971 Act

4.—(1)   Subject to sub-paragraphs (3) and (4) of this paragraph and to paragraph 5 below, the provisions of the 1971 Act specified in sub-paragraph (2) below shall have effect as if section 8 of this Act were contained in Part II of that Act.

(2)   The provisions referred to in sub-paragraph (1) above are—

(a)   section 18 (notice of decisions appealable under that Part and statement of appeal rights etc);

(b)   section 19 (determination of appeals under that Part by adjudicators);

(c)   section 20 (appeal from adjudicator to Immigration Appeal Tribunal);

(d)   section 21 (references of cases by Secretary of State for further consideration);

(e)   section 22(1) to (4), (6) and (7) (rules of procedure for appeals);

(f)   section 23 (grants to voluntary organisations helping persons with rights of appeal);

(ff)   section 33(4) duration of appeals); and

(g)   Schedule 5 (provisions about adjudicators and Immigration Appeal Tribunal).

(3)   Rules of procedure under section 22 may make special provision in relation to—

(a)   proceedings on appeals on any of the grounds mentioned in subsections (1) to (4) of section 8 of this Act; and

(b)   proceedings in which, by virtue of paragraph 3 above, a special adjudicator is required to deal both with an appeal on any of those grounds and another appeal.

(4)   So much of paragraph 5 of Schedule 5 as relates to the allocation of duties among the adjudicators shall have effect subject to subsection (5) of section 8 of this Act.

Asylum claims — extension of special appeals procedures

SPECIAL APPEALS PROCEDURES FOR CLAIMS WITHOUT FOUNDATION

5.—(1)   This paragraph applies to an appeal by a person on any of the grounds mentioned in subsections (1) to (4) of section 8 of this Act if the Secretary of State has certified that, in his opinion, the person's claim on the ground that it would be contrary to the United Kingdom's obligations under the Convention for him to be removed from, or be required to leave, the United Kingdom is one to which—

(a)   sub-paragraph (2), (3) or (4) below applies; and

(b)   sub-paragraph (5) below does not apply.

(2)   This sub-paragraph applies to a claim if the country or territory to which the appellant is to be sent is designated in an order made by the Secretary of State by statutory instrument as a country or territory in which it appears to him that there is in general no serious risk of persecution.

(3)   This sub-paragraph applies to a claim if, on his arrival in the United Kingdom, the appellant was required by an immigration officer to produce a valid passport and either—

(a)   he failed to produce a passport without giving a reasonable explanation for his failure to do so; or

(b)   he produced a passport which was not in fact valid and failed to inform the officer of that fact.

(4)   This sub-paragraph applies to a claim if—

(a)   it does not show a fear of persecution by reason of the appellant's race, religion, nationality, membership of a particular social group, or political opinion;

(b)   it shows a fear of such persecution, but the fear is manifestly unfounded or the circumstances which gave rise to the fear no longer subsist;

(c)   it is made at any time after the appellant—

(i)   has been refused leave to enter under the 1971 Act,

(ii)   has been recommended for deportation by a court empowered by that Act to do so,

(iii)   has been notified of the Secretary of State's decision to make a deportation order against him by virtue of section 3(5) of that Act, or

(iv)   has been notified of his liability to removal under paragraph 9 of Schedule 2 to that Act;

(d)   it is manifestly fraudulent, or any of the evidence adduced in its support is manifestly false; or

(e)   it is frivolous or vexatious.

(5)   This sub-paragraph applies to a claim if the evidence adduced in its support establishes a reasonable likelihood that the appellant has been tortured in the country or territory to which he is to be sent.

(6)   Rules of procedure under section 22 of the 1971 Act may make special provision in relation to appeals to which this paragraph applies.

(7)   If on appeal to which this paragraph applies the special adjudicator agrees that the claim is one to which—

(a)   sub-paragraph (2), (3) or (4) above applies; and

(b)   sub-paragraph (5) above does not apply,

section 20(1) of that Act shall confer on the appellant any right to appeal to the Immigration Appeal Tribunal.

(8)   The first order under this paragraph shall not be made unless a draft of the order has been laid before and approved by a resolution of each House of Parliament.

(9)   A statutory instrument containing a subsequent order under this paragraph shall be subject to annulment in pursuance of a resolution of either House of Parliament.

(10)   In this paragraph—
'immigration officer' means an immigration officer appointed for the purposes of the 1971 Act;
'passport', in relation to an appellant, means a passport with photograph or some other document satisfactorily establishing his identity and nationality or citizenship'.

Exception for national security

6.   Subsection (5) of section 13, subsection (3) of section 14 and subsections (3) and (4) of section 15 of the 1971 Act shall have effect in relation to the rights of appeal conferred by section 8(1), (2) and (3) (a) and (b) of this Act respectively as they have effect in relation to the rights of appeal conferred by subsection (1) of those sections of that Act but as if references to a person's exclusion, departure of deportation being conducive to the public good were references to its being in the interests of national security.

Suspension of variation of limited leave pending appeal

7.   The limitation on the taking effect of a variation and on a requirement to leave the United Kingdom contained in subsection (1) of section 14 of the 1971 Act shall have effect as if appeals under section 8(2) of this Act were appeals under that subsection.

Deportation order not to be made while appeal pending

8.   In section 15(2) of the 1971 Act references to an appeal against a decision to make a deportation order shall include references to an appeal against such a decision under section 8(3)(a) of this Act.

Stay of removal directions pending appeal and bail

9.   Part II of Schedule 2 and paragraph 3 of Schedule 3, to the 1971 Act shall have effect as if the references to appeals under section 13(1), 15(1)(a) and 16 of that Act included (respectively) appeals under section 8(1), (3) and (4) of this Act and as if sub-paragraph (5) of paragraph 28 of Schedule 2 were omitted.

SOCIAL SECURITY

The Social Security (Persons From Abroad) Miscellaneous Amendments Regulations 1996 (SI 1996, No. 30)

Made – – – – –	*11th January 1996*
Laid before Parliament	*11th January 1996*
Coming into force	*5th February 1996*

The Secretary of State for Social Security, in exercise of powers conferred upon him by sections 64(1), 68(4)(c)(i), 70(4), 71(6), 123(1), 124(1), 128(1), 129(1), 130(1) and (2), 131(1) and (3), 135, 137(1) and (2)(a) and (i) and 175(1) and (3) to (5) of the Social Security Contributions and Benefits Act 1992(a) and section 5(1)(r) of the Social Security Administration Act 1992(b) and of all other powers enabling him in that behalf, and so far as they relate to housing benefit and council tax benefit after consultation with organisations appearing to him to be representative of the authorities concerned(c), and after reference to the Social Security Advisory Committee(d), hereby makes the following Regulations:–

1. Citation, commencement and interpretation

(1) These Regulations may be cited as the Social Security (Persons From Abroad) Miscellaneous Amendments Regulations 1996 and shall come into force on 5 February 1996.

(a) 1992 c. 4; sections 123(1)(e) and 131 of the Social Security Contributions and Benefits Act 1992 were substituted by the Local Government Finance Act 1992 (c. 14), section 103 and Schedule 9, paragraphs 1(1) and 4. Section 137(1) which is an interpretation provision is cited because of the meaning assigned to the word 'prescribed'.
(b) 1992 c. 5.
(c) *See* the Social Security Administration Act 1992 (c. 5), section 176(1).
(d) *See* the Social Security Administration Act 1992 (c. 5), section 172(1).

(2)   In these Regulations, unless the context otherwise requires—
'the Attendance Allowance Regulations' means the Social Security (Attendance Allowance) Regulations 1991(**e**);
'the Council Tax Benefit Regulations' means the Council Tax Benefit (General) Regulations 1992(**f**);
'the Disability Living Allowance Regulations' means the Social Security (Disability Living Allowance) Regulations 1991(**g**);
'the Disability Working Allowance Regulations' means the Disability Working Allowance (General) Regulations 1991(**h**);
'the Family Credit Regulations' means the Family Credit (General) Regulations 1987(**i**);
'the Housing Benefit Regulations' means the Housing Benefit (General) Regulations 1987(**j**);
'the Invalid Care Allowance Regulations' means the Social Security (Invalid Care Allowance) Regulations 1976(**a**);
'the Income Support Regulations' means the Income Support (General) Regulations 1987(**b**);
'the Payments on Account, Overpayments and Recovery Regulations' means the Social Security (Payments on account, Overpayments and Recovery) Regulations 1988(**c**);
'the Severe Disablement Allowance Regulations' means the Social Security (Severe Disablement Allowance) Regulations 1984(**d**).

2.   Amendment of regulation 2 of the Attendance Allowance Regulations

In regulation 2 of the Attendance Allowance Regulations (conditions as to residence and presence in Great Britain)—
   (a)   after paragraph (1)(a)(i) there shall be inserted—
      '(ia)   subject to paragraph (1A), his right to reside or remain in Great Britain is not subject to any limitation or condition, and'; and
   (b)   after paragraph (1) there shall be inserted—
      '(1A)   For the purposes of paragraph (1)(a)(ia), a person's right to reside or remain in Great Britain is not to be treated as if it were subject to a limitation or condition if—
         (a)   he is a person recorded by the Secretary of State as a refugee within the definition in Article 1 of the Convention relating to the Status of Refugees

(e) S.I. 1991/2740, to which there are amendments not relevant to this regulation.
(f) S.I. 1992/1814, to which there are amendments not relevant to this regulation.
(g) S.I. 1991/2890, to which there are amendments not relevant to this regulation.
(h) S.I. 1991/2887, to which there are amendments not relevant to this regulation.
(i) S.I. 1987/1973, to which there are amendments not relevant to this regulation.
(j) S.I. 1987/1971, to which there are amendments not relevant to this regulation.
(a) S.I. 1976/409, to which there are amendments not relevant to this regulation.
(b) S.I. 1987/1967, to which there are amendments not relevant to this regulation.
(c) S.I. 1988/664, to which there are amendments not relevant to this regulation.
(d) S.I. 1984/1303, to which there are amendments not relevant to this regulation.

done at Geneva on 28 July 1951(e), as extended by Article 1(2) of the Protocol relating to the Status of Refugees done at New York on 31 January 1967(f);

(b) he is a person who has been granted exceptional leave outside the provisions of the immigration rules within the meaning of the Immigration Act 1971(g) to remain in the United Kingdom by the Secretary of State;

(c) he is a national, or a member of the family of a national, of a State contracting party to the Agreement on the European Economic Area signed at Oporto on 2 May 1992 as adjusted by the Protocol signed at Brussels on 17 March 1993(h);

(d) he is a person who is—

(i) lawfully working in Great Britain and is a national of a State with which the Community has concluded an Agreement under article 238(i) of the Treaty establishing the European Community(j) providing, in the field of social security, for the equal treatment of workers who are nationals of the signatory State and their families, or

(ii) a member of the family of, and living with, such a person; or

(e) he is a person in respect of whom there is an Order in Council under section 179 of the Social Security Administration Act 1992(k) giving effect to a reciprocal agreement which, for the purposes of attendance allowance, has the effect that periods of presence or residence in another country are to be treated as periods of presence or residence in Great Britain.'.

3. Amendment of regulation 4A of the Council Tax Benefit Regulations

In regulation 4A of the Council Tax Benefit Regulations(a) (persons from abroad)—

(a) after paragraph (4)(e) there shall be added—

'; or

(f) has been given leave to enter, or remain in, the United Kingdom by the Secretary of State upon an undertaking given by another person or persons in writing in pursuance of immigration rules within the meaning of the 1971 Act, to be responsible for his maintenance and accommodation; and he has not been resident in the United Kingdom for a period of at least 5 years beginning from the date of entry or the date on which the undertaking was given in respect of him, whichever date is the later; or

(g) while he is a person to whom any of the definitions in paragraph (2) or sub-paragraphs (a) to (d) and (f) of this paragraph applies, submits a claim to the Secretary of State, which is not finally determined, for asylum under the Convention relating to the Status of Refugees.';

(e) Cmd. 9171.
(f) Cmnd. 3906.
(g) 1971 c. 77.
(h) OJ No. L 1, 3.1.1994, p. 7.
(i) Article 238 was amended by article G(84) of the Treaty on European Union.
(j) The title of the Treaty of Rome was amended by Article G(1) of the Treaty on European Union.
(k) 1992 c. 5.
(a) Regulation 4A was inserted by S.I. 1994/470 and further amended by S.I. 1994/1807.

(b)   for paragraph (5) there shall be substituted—

'(5)   This paragraph applies to a person who—

(a) is an asylum seeker and for this purpose a person is an asylum seeker when he submits on his arrival (other than on his re-entry) in the United Kingdom from a country outside the Common Travel Area a claim for asylum to the Secretary of State that it would be contrary to the United Kingdom's obligations under the Convention relating to the Status of Refugees for him to be removed from, or required to leave, the United Kingdom and that claim is recorded by the Secretary of State as having been made; or

(b) becomes, while present in Great Britain, an asylum seeker and for this purpose a person is an asylum seeker when—

(i) the Secretary of State makes a declaration to the effect that the country of which he is a national is subject to such a fundamental change in circumstances that he would not normally order the return of a person to that country, and

(ii) he submits, within a period of 3 months from the day that declaration was made, a claim for asylum to the Secretary of State under the Convention relating to the Status of Refugees, and

(iii) his claim for asylum under that Convention is recorded by the Secretary of State as having been made; or

(c) is a person to whom paragraph (4)(f) (sponsored immigrant) applies and the person or persons who gave the undertaking to provide for his maintenance and accommodation has, or as the case may be have, died; or

(d) is in receipt of income support.';

(c)   after paragraph (5) there shall be inserted—

'(5A) For the purposes of paragraph (5)(a) and (b), a person ceases to be an asylum seeker—

(a) in the case of a claim for asylum which, on or after 5 February 1996, is recorded by the Secretary of State as having been determined (other than on appeal) or abandoned, on the date on which it is so recorded, or

(b) in the case of a claim for asylum which is recorded as determined before 5 February 1996 and in respect of which there is either an appeal pending on 5 February 1996 or an appeal is made within the time limits specified in rule 5 of the Asylum Appeals (Procedure) Rules 1993(a), on the date on which that appeal is determined.'; and

(d) in paragraph (7) after the definition of 'the 1971 Act' there shall be inserted—

'"the Common Travel Area" means the United Kingdom, the Channel Islands, the Isle of Man and the Republic of Ireland collectively;

"the Convention relating to the Status of Refugees" means the Convention relating to the Status of Refugees done at Geneva on 28 July 1951(b), as

---

(a) S.I. 1993/1661.
(b) Cmd. 9171.

extended by Article 1(2) of the Protocol relating to the Status of Refugees done at New York on 31 January 1967(c);'.

4. Amendment of regulation 2 of the Disability Living Allowance Regulations

In regulation 2 of the Disability Living Allowance Regulations(d) (conditions as to residence and presence in Great Britain)—

(a)   after paragraph (1)(a)(i) there shall be inserted—

'(ia)   subject to paragraph (1A), his right to reside or remain in Great Britain is not subject to any limitation or condition, and'; and

(b)   after paragraph (1) there shall be inserted—

'(1A)   For the purposes of paragraph (l)(a)(ia), a person's right to reside or remain in Great Britain is not to be treated as if it were subject to a limitation or condition if—

(a)   he is a person recorded by the Secretary of State as a refugee within the definition in Article 1 of the Convention relating to the Status
of Refugees done at Geneva on 28 July 1951(e), as extended by Article 1(2) of the Protocol relating to the Status of Refugees done at New York on 31 January 1967(f);

(b)   he is a person who has been granted exceptional leave outside the provisions of the immigration rules within the meaning of the Immigration Act 1971(g) to remain in the United Kingdom by the Secretary of State;

(c)   he is a national, or a member of the family of a national, of a State contracting party to the Agreement on the European Economic Area signed at Oporto on 2 May 1992 as adjusted by the Protocol signed at Brussels on 17 March 1993(h);

(d)   he is a person who is—

(i)   lawfully working in Great Britain and is a national of a State with which the Community has concluded an Agreement under article 238(i) of the Treaty establishing the European Community(j) providing, in the field of social security, for the equal treatment of workers who are nationals of the signatory State and their families, or

(ii)   a member of the family of, and living with, such a person; or

(e)   he is a person in respect of whom there is an Order in Council under section 179 of the Administration Act 1992 giving effect to a reciprocal agreement which, for the purposes of disability living allowance, has the effect that periods of presence or residence in another country are to be treated as periods of presence or residence in Great Britain.'.

(c) Cmnd. 3906.
(d) Regulation 2 was amended by S.I. 1993/1939.
(e) Cmd. 9171.
(f) Cmnd. 3906.
(g) 1971 c. 77.
(h) OJ No. L 1, 3.1.1994, p. 7.
(i) Article 238 was amended by article G(84) of the Treaty on European Union.
(j) The title of the Treaty of Rome was amended by Article G(1) of the Treaty on European Union.

5. Amendment of regulation 5 of the Disability Working Allowance Regulations

In regulation 5 of the Disability Working Allowance Regulations (circumstances in which a person is treated as being or as not being in Great Britain)—

(a) after paragraph (1)(a) there shall be inserted—

'(aa) subject to paragraph (1A), his right to reside or remain in Great Britain is not subject to any limitation or condition; and'; and

(b) after paragraph (1) there shall be inserted—

'(1A) For the purposes of paragraph (1)(aa), a person's right to reside or remain in Great Britain is not to be treated as if it were subject to a limitation or condition if—

(a) he is a person recorded by the Secretary of State as a refugee within the definition in Article 1 of the Convention relating to the Status of Refugees done at Geneva on 28 July 1951(a), as extended by Article 1(2) of the Protocol relating to the Status of Refugees done at New York on 31 January 1967(b);

(b) he is a person who has been granted exceptional leave outside the provisions of the immigration rules within the meaning of the Immigration Act 1971(c) to remain in the United Kingdom by the Secretary of State;

(c) he is a national, or a member of the family of a national, of a State contracting party to the Agreement on the European Economic Area signed at Oporto on 2 May 1992 as adjusted by the Protocol signed at Brussels on 17 March 1993(d); or

(d) he is a person who is—

(i) lawfully working in Great Britain and is a national of a State with which the Community has concluded an Agreement under article 238(e) of the Treaty establishing the European Community(f) providing, in the field of social security, for the equal treatment of workers who are nationals of the signatory State and their families, or

(ii) a member of the family of, and living with, such a person.'.

6. Amendment of regulation 3 of the Family Credit Regulations

In regulation 3 of the Family Credit Regulations(g) (circumstances in which a person is treated as being or as not being in Great Britain)—

(a) after paragraph (1)(a) there shall be inserted—

'(aa) subject to paragraph (1A), his right to reside or remain in Great Britain is not subject to any limitation or condition, and'; and

(b) after paragraph (1) there shall be inserted—

(a) Cmd. 9171.
(b) Cmnd. 3906.
(c) 1971 c. 77.
(d) OJ No. L 1, 3.1.1994, p. 7.
(e) Article 238 was amended by article G(84) of the Treaty on European Union.
(f) The title of the Treaty of Rome was amended by Article G(1) of the Treaty on European Union.
(g) Regulation 3 was a amended by S.I. 1991/2742.

'(1A) For the purposes of paragraph (1)(aa), a person's right to reside or remain in Great Britain is not to be treated as if it were subject to a limitation or condition if—

(a) he is a person recorded by the Secretary of State as a refugee within the definition in Article 1 of the Convention relating to the Status of Refugees done at Geneva on 28 July 1951(**h**), as extended by Article 1(2) of the Protocol relating to the Status of Refugees done at New York on 31 January 1967(**i**);

(b) he is a person who has been granted exceptional leave outside the provisions of the immigration rules within the meaning of the Immigration Act 1971(**a**) to remain in the United Kingdom by the Secretary of State;

(c) he is a national, or a member of the family of a national, of a State contracting party to the Agreement on the European Economic Area signed at Oporto on 2 May 1992 as adjusted by the Protocol signed at Brussels on 17 March 1993(**b**); or

(d) he is a person who is—

(i) lawfully working in Great Britain and is a national of a State with which the Community has concluded an Agreement under article 238(**c**) of the Treaty establishing the European Community(**d**) providing, in the field of social security, for the equal treatment of workers who are nationals of the signatory State and their families, or

(ii) a member of the family of, and living with, such a person.'.

7. Amendment of regulation 7A of the Housing Benefit Regulations

In regulation 7A of the Housing Benefit Regulations(**e**) (persons from abroad)—

(a) after paragraph (4)(e) there shall be added—

'; or

(f) has been given leave to enter, or remain in, the United Kingdom by the Secretary of State upon an undertaking given by another person or persons in writing in pursuance of immigration rules within the meaning of the 1971 Act, to be responsible for his maintenance and accommodation; and he has not been resident in the United Kingdom for a period of at least 5 years beginning from the date of entry or the date on which the undertaking was given in respect of him, whichever date is the later; or

(g) while he is a person to whom any of the definitions in paragraph (2) or sub-paragraphs (a) to (d) and (f) of this paragraph applies, submits a claim to the Secretary of State, which is not finally determined, for asylum under the Convention relating to the Status of Refugees.';

(**h**) Cmd. 9171.
(**i**) Cmnd. 3906.
(**a**) 1971 c. 77.
(**b**) OJ No. L 1, 3.1.1994, p. 7.
(**c**) Article 238 was amended by article G(84) of the Treaty on European Union.
(**d**) The title of the Treaty of Rome was amended by Article G(1) of the Treaty on European Union.
(**e**) Regulation 7A was inserted by S.I. 1994/470 and further amended by S.I. 1994/1807.

(b)   for paragraph (5) there shall be substituted—

'(5)   This paragraph applies to a person who—

(a)   is an asylum seeker and for this purpose a person is an asylum seeker when he submits on his arrival (other than on his re-entry) in the United Kingdom from a country outside the Common Travel Area a claim for asylum to the Secretary of State that it would be contrary to the United Kingdom's obligations under the Convention relating to the Status of Refugees for him to be removed from, or required to leave, the United Kingdom and that claim is recorded by the Secretary of State as having been made; or

(b)   becomes, while present in Great Britain, an asylum seeker and for this purpose a person is an asylum seeker when—

(i)   the Secretary of State makes a declaration to the effect that the country of which he is a national is subject to such a fundamental change in circumstances that he would not normally order the return of a person to that country, and

(ii)   he submits, within a period of 3 months from the day that declaration was made, a claim for asylum to the Secretary of State under the Convention relating to the Status of Refugees, and

(iii)   his claim for asylum under that Convention is recorded by the Secretary of State as having been made; or

(c)   is a person to whom paragraph (4)(f) (sponsored immigrant) applies and the person or persons who gave the undertaking to provide for his maintenance and accommodation has, or as the case may be have, died; or

(d)   is in receipt of income support.';

(c)   after paragraph (5) there shall be inserted—

'(5A)   For the purposes of paragraph (5)(a) and (b), a person ceases to be an asylum seeker—

(a)   in the case of a claim for asylum which, on or after 5 February 1996, is recorded by the Secretary of State as having been determined (other than on appeal) or abandoned, on the date on which it is so recorded, or

(b)   in the case of a claim for asylum which is recorded as determined before 5 February 1996 and in respect of which there is either an appeal pending on 5 February 1996 or an appeal is made within the time limits specified in rule 5 of the Asylum Appeals (Procedure) Rules 1993(a), on the date on which that appeal is determined.'; and

(d)   in paragraph (7) after the definition of 'the 1971 Act' there shall be inserted—

'"the Common Travel Area" means the United Kingdom, the Channel Islands, the Isle of Man and the Republic of Ireland collectively;

"the Convention relating to the Status of Refugees" means the Convention relating to the Status of Refugees done at Geneva on 28 July 1951(b), as

---

(a) S.I. 1993/1661.
(b) Cmd. 9171.

extended by Article 1(2) of the Protocol relating to the Status of Refugees done at New York on 31st January 1967(**c**);'.

8. Amendment of the Income Support Regulations

(1) The Income Support Regulations shall be amended in accordance with the following paragraphs of this regulation.

(2) In regulation 21(3)(**d**) in the definition of 'person from abroad', after sub-paragraph (h) there shall be added—

'; or

(i) has been given leave to enter, or remain in, the United Kingdom by the Secretary of State upon an undertaking given by another person or persons in writing in pursuance of immigration rules within the meaning of the Immigration Act 1971(**e**), to be responsible for his maintenance and accommodation; and he has not been resident in the United Kingdom for a period of at least 5 years beginning from the date of entry or the date on which the undertaking was given in respect of him, whichever date is the later, or

(j) while he is a person to whom any of the definitions in sub-paragraphs (a) to (i) applies in his case, submits a claim to the Secretary of State, which is not finally determined, for asylum under the Convention(**f**);'.

(3) In regulation 70 (urgent cases)—

(a) for sub-paragraph (c) of paragraph (3) there shall be substituted—

'(c) is a person to whom sub-paragraph (i) of that definition (sponsored immigrant) applies and the person or persons who gave the undertaking to provide for his maintenance and accommodation has, as the case may be have, died;';

(b) sub-paragraphs (e) to (j) of paragraph (3)(**a**) shall be omitted;

(c) for sub-paragraph (a) of paragraph (3A)(**b**) there shall be substituted—

'(a) is an asylum seeker when he submits on his arrival (other than on his re-entry) in the United Kingdom from a country outside the Common Travel Area a claim for asylum to the Secretary of State that it would be contrary to the United Kingdom's obligations under the Convention for him to be removed from, or required to leave, the United Kingdom and that claim is recorded by the Secretary of State as having been made; or

(aa) becomes, while present in Great Britain, an asylum seeker when—

(i) the Secretary of State makes a declaration to the effect that the country of which he is a national is subject to such a fundamental change in

(**c**) Cmnd. 3906.

(**d**) Paragraph 3 was amended by S.I. 1990/547, 1991/236, 1992/3147, 1993/315, 1994/1807 and 2139 and 1995/516.

(**e**) 1971 c. 77 as amended by the British Nationality Act 1981 (c. 61).

(**f**) The Convention relating to the Status of Refugees done at Geneva on 28 July 1951 and the Protocol to that Convention.

(**a**) Sub-paragraph (d) of paragraph (3) was omitted by S.I. 1993/1679.

(**b**) Paragraph (3A) was inserted by S.I. 1993/1679.

circumstances that he would not normally order the return of a person to that country, and

(ii) he submits, within a period of 3 months from the day that declaration was made, a claim for asylum to the Secretary of State under the Convention relating to the Status of Refugees, and

(iii) his claim for asylum under that Convention is recorded by the Secretary of State as having been made; and';

(d) for sub-paragraph (b) of paragraph (3A) there shall be substituted—

'(b) ceases to be an asylum seeker—

(i) in the case of a claim for asylum which, on or after 5 February 1996, is recorded by the Secretary of State as having been determined (other than on appeal) or abandoned, on the date on which it is so recorded, or

(ii) in the case of a claim for asylum which is recorded as determined before 5 February 1996 and in respect of which there is either an appeal pending on 5 February 1996 or an appeal is made within the time limits specified in rule 5 of the Asylum Appeals (Procedure) Rules 1993(c), on the date on which that appeal is determined.'; and

(e) in paragraph (3B), at the end there shall be added—

'; and "the Common Travel Area" means the United Kingdom, the Channel Islands, the Isle of Man and the Republic of Ireland collectively.'.

(4) In regulation 71 (applicable amounts in urgent cases), sub-paragraphs (b) to (f) of paragraph (2) shall be omitted.

9. Amendment of regulation 9 of the Invalid Care Allowance Regulations

In regulation 9 of the Invalid Care Allowance Regulations(d) (conditions relating to residence and presence in Great Britain)—

(a) after paragraph (1)(a) shall be inserted—

'(aa) subject to paragraph (1A), his right to reside or remain in Great Britain is not subject to any limitation or condition, and'; and

(b) after paragraph (1) there shall be inserted—

'(1A) For the purposes of paragraph (1)(aa), a person's right to reside or remain in Great Britain is not to be treated as if it were subject to a limitation or condition if—

(a) he is a person recorded by the Secretary of State as a refugee within the definition in Article 1 of the Convention relating to the Status of Refugees done at Geneva on 28 July 1951(e), as extended by Article 1(2) of the Protocol relating to the Status of Refugees done at New York on 31 January 1967(a);

(b) he is a person who has been granted exceptional leave outside the provisions of the immigration rules within the meaning of the Immigration Act 1971(b) to remain in the United Kingdom by the Secretary of State;

(c) S.I. 1993/1661.
(d) Regulation 9 was amended by S.I. 1977/342 and 1991/2742.
(e) Cmd. 9171.
(a) Cmnd. 3906.
(b) 1971 c. 77.

(c)   he is a national, or a member of the family of a national, of a State contracting party to the Agreement on the European Economic Area signed at Oporto on 2 May 1992 as adjusted by the Protocol signed at Brussels on 17 March 1993(**c**); or

(d)   he is a person who is—

(i)   lawfully working in Great Britain and is a national of a State with which the Community has concluded an Agreement under article 238(**d**) of the Treaty establishing the European Community(**e**) providing, in the field of social security, for the equal treatment of workers who are nationals of the signatory State and their families, or

(ii)   a member of the family of, and living with, such a person.'.

10.   Amendment of regulation 2 of the Payments on Account, Overpayments and Recovery Regulations

In regulation 2 of the Payments on Account, Overpayments and Recovery Regulations(**f**) (making of interim payments)—

(a)   in paragraph (1), at the beginning there shall be inserted the words 'Subject to paragraph (1A),';

(b)   after paragraph (1) there shall be inserted—

'(1A)   Paragraph (1) shall not apply pending the determination of an appeal unless the Secretary of State is of the opinion that there is entitlement to benefit.'.

11.   Amendment of regulation 3 of the Severe Disablement Allowance Regulations

In regulation 3 of the Severe Disablement Allowance Regulations(**g**) (conditions relating to residence and presence)—

(a)   after paragraph (1)(a)(i) there shall be inserted—

'(ia)   subject to paragraph (1B), his right to reside or remain in Great Britain is not subject to any limitation or condition, and'; and

(b)   after paragraph (1A) there shall be inserted—

'(1B)   For the purposes of paragraph (1)(a)(ia), a person's right to reside or remain in Great Britain is not to be treated as if it were subject to a limitation or condition if—

(a)   he is a person recorded by the Secretary of State as a refugee within the definition in Article 1 of the Convention relating to the Status of Refugees done at Geneva on 28 July 1951(**h**), as extended by Article 1(2) of the Protocol relating to the Status of Refugees done at New York on 31 January 1967(**i**);

(c) OJ No. L 1, 3.1.1994, p. 7.
(d) Article 238 was amended by article G(84) of the Treaty on European Union.
(e) The title of the Treaty of Rome was amended by Article G(1) of the Treaty on European Union.
(f) Regulation 2 was amended by S.I. 1991/2742 and 1993/650.
(g) Regulation 3 was amended by S.I. 1991/1747, 1992/704 and 1994/2947.
(h) Cmd. 9171.
(i) Cmnd. 3906.

(b)   he is a person who has been granted exceptional leave outside the provisions of the immigration rules within the meaning of the Immigration Act 1971(a) to remain in the United Kingdom by the Secretary of State;

(c)   he is a national, or a member of the family of a national, of a State contracting party to the Agreement on the European Economic Area signed at Oporto on 2 May 1992 as adjusted by the Protocol signed at Brussels on 17 March 1993(b); or

(d)   he is a person who is—

(i)   lawfully working in Great Britain and is a national of a State with which the Community has concluded an Agreement under article 238(c) of the Treaty establishing the European Community(d) providing, in the field of social security, for the equal treatment of workers who are nationals of the signatory State and their families, or

(ii)   a member of the family of, and living with, such a person.'

12. Saving

(1)   Where, before the coming into force of these Regulations, a person who becomes an asylum seeker under regulation 4A(5)(a)(i) of the Council Tax Benefit Regulations, regulation 7A(5)(a)(i) of the Housing Benefit Regulations or regulation 70(3A)(a) of the Income Support Regulations, as the case may be, is entitled to benefit under any of those Regulations, those provisions of those Regulations as then in force shall continue to have effect as if regulations 3(a) and (b), 7(a) and (b) or 8(2) and (3)(c), as the case may be, of these Regulations had not been made.

(2)   Where, before the coming into force of these Regulations, a person, in respect of whom an undertaking was given by another person or persons to be responsible for his maintenance and accommodation, claimed benefit to which he is entitled, or is receiving benefit, under the Council Tax Benefit Regulations, the Housing Benefit Regulations or the Income Support Regulations, as the case may be, those Regulations as then in force shall have effect as if regulations 3, 7 or 8, as the case may be, of these Regulations had not been made.

(3)   Where, before the coming into force of these Regulations, a person is receiving attendance allowance, disability living allowance, disability working allowance, family credit, invalid care allowance or severe disablement allowance under, as the case may be, the Attendance Allowance Regulations, Disability Living Allowance Regulations, Disability Working Allowance Regulations, Family Credit Regulations, Invalid Care Allowance Regulations or Severe Disablement Allowance Regulations, those Regulations shall, until such time as his entitlement to that benefit is reviewed under section 25 or 30 of the Social Security Administration Act 1992(e), have effect as if regulation 2, 4, 5, 6, 9 or 11, as the case may be, of these Regulations had not been made.

(a) 1971 c. 77.
(b) OJ No L 1, 3.1.1994, p. 7.
(c) Article 238 was amended by article G(84) of the Treaty on European Union.
(d) The title of the Treaty of Rome was amended by Article G(1) of the Treaty on European Union.
(e) 1992 c. 5.

Signed by authority of the Secretary of State for Social Security.

Roger Evans
Parliamentary Under-Secretary of State,
11 January 1996   Department of Social Security

EXPLANATORY NOTE

(This note is not part of the Regulations)

These Regulations further amend the Social Security (Attendance Allowance) Regulations 1991 (SI 1991/2740), the Council Tax Benefit (General) Regulations 1992 (SI 1992/1814), the Social Security (Disability Living Allowance) Regulations 1991 (SI 1991/2890), the Disability Working Allowance (General) Regulations 1991 (SI1991/2887), the Family Credit (General) Regulations 1987 (SI 1987/1973), the Housing Benefit (General) Regulations 1987 (SI 1987/1971), the Social Security (Invalid Care Allowance) Regulations 1976 (SI 1976/409), the Income Support (General) Regulations 1987 (SI 1987/1967), the Social Security (Payments on account, Overpayments and Recovery) Regulations 1988 (SI 1988/664) and the Social Security (Severe Disablement Allowance) Regulations 1984 (SI 1984/1303).

These Regulations exclude a person from entitlement to certain non-contributory benefits if his right to reside or remain in Great Britain is subject to any limitation or condition (regulations 2, 4, 5, 6, 9, and 11); make provision regarding interim payments in the course of an appeal (regulation 10); make provision in respect of asylum seekers and sponsored immigrants who, except in certain circumstances, are denied income related benefits (regulations 3, 7 and 8); and make saving provisions (regulation 12).

These Regulations do not impose a charge on business.

The Report of the Social Security Advisory Committee dated 8 December 1995 on the proposals referred to them, together with a statement showing the extent to which these Regulations give effect to the Report and in so far as they do not give effect to it, the reasons why not, are contained in Command Paper Cm. 3062, published by Her Majesty's Stationery Office.

HOUSING ENGLAND AND WALES
HOUSING SCOTLAND

The Housing Accommodation and Homelessness (Persons subject to Immigration Control) Order 1996 (SI 1966 No. 1982)

Made	*29th July 1996*
Laid before Parliament	*29th July 1996*
Coming into force	*19th August 1996*

The Secretary of State, in exercise of the powers conferred on him by section 9 of the Asylum and Immigration Act 1996 (a) and of all other powers enabling him in that behalf, hereby makes the following Order—

1. Citation, commencement and extent

(1) This Order may be cited as the Housing Accommodation and Homelessness (Persons subject to Immigration Control) Order 1996 and shall come into force on 19 August 1996.

(2) This Order does not extend to Northern Ireland.

2. Interpretation

In this Order—

'the Act' means the Asylum and Immigration Act 1996;

'the 1971 Act **(b)**' means the Immigration Act 1971;

'claim for asylum' means a claim made by a person that it would be contrary to the United Kingdom's obligations under the Convention for him to be removed from or required to leave the United Kingdom;

(a) 1996 c.49.
(b) 1971 c. 77.

'Common Travel Area' means the United Kingdom, the Channel Islands, the Isle of Man and the Republic of Ireland collectively;

'the Convention' means the Convention relating to the Status of Refugees done at Geneva on 28th July 1951 (c), as extended by Article 1(2) of the Protocol relating to the Status of Refugees done at New York on 31 January 1967 (d);

'full time course' means a course normally involving not less than 15 hours attendance a week in term time for the organised day-time study of a single subject or related subjects;

'overseas student' means a person who is attending a full-time course at a specified education institution;

'specified education institution' means—

(a)   a university or other institution within the higher education sector within the meaning given by section 91(5) of the Further and Higher Education Act 1992 (a) or by section 56(2) of the Further and Higher Education (Scotland) Act 1992 (b);

(b)   an institution within the further education sector within the meaning given by section 91(3) of the Further and Higher Education Act 1992;

(c)   a college of further education in Scotland which is under the management of an education authority or which is managed by a board of management in terms of Part I of the Further and Higher Education (Scotland) Act 1992;

(d)   a central institution within the meaning of section 135(1) of the Education (Scotland) Act 1980 (c);

(e)   an institution which provides a course qualifying for funding under Part I of the Education Act 1994 (d).

3.   Classes specified under section 9(1)

The following are the classes of persons specified for the purposes of section 9(1) of the Act—

Class A – a person recorded by the Secretary of State as a refugee within the definition in Article 1 of the Convention;

Class B – a person—

(i)   who has been granted by the Secretary of State exceptional leave to enter or remain in the United Kingdom outside the provisions of the immigration rules within the meaning of the 1971 Act; and

(ii)   whose leave is not subject to a condition requiring him to maintain and accommodate himself and any dependants of his without recourse to public funds;

Class C – a person who has a current leave to enter or remain in the United Kingdom which is not subject to any limitation or condition;

(c) Cmd 9171.
(d) Cmd 3906.
(a) 1992 c. 13.
(b) 1992 c. 37.
(c) 1980 c. 44.
(d) 1994 c. 30.

Class D – an overseas student in a case where the housing accommodation which is or may be provided to him—

(a)   is let by a housing authority to a specified education institution for the purposes of enabling that institution to provide accommodation for students attending a full time course at that institution; and

(b)   would otherwise be difficult for that authority to let on satisfactory terms.

4.   Classes specified under section 9(2)

The classes of persons specified for the purposes of section 9(2) of the Act are those specified in classes A to C of article 3 and—

Class E – a person who has made a claim for asylum which is recorded by the Secretary of State as having been made either—

(i)   on his arrival (other than on his re-entry) in the United Kingdom from a country outside the Common Travel Area; or

(ii)   within 3 months from the day on which the Secretary of State makes a declaration to the effect that the country of which he is a national is subject to such a fundamental change in circumstances that he would not normally order the return of a person to that country,

and which in either case, has not been recorded by the Secretary of State as having been determined or abandoned;

Class F – a person (other than a person falling within Class E) who on or before 4th February 1996 has made a claim for asylum and who was on that date entitled to benefit under the Housing Benefit (General) Regulations 1987 **(a)** in a case where—

(i)   his claim has not been recorded by the Secretary of State as having been determined or abandoned; or

(ii)   there was on that date an appeal pending in respect of that claim or such an appeal is made within the time limits specified in rules of procedure made under section 22 of the 1971 Act,

and, in either case, no determination or abandoning of the appeal in question has been recorded by the Secretary of State since that date.

Signed by authority of the Secretary of State

Paul Beresford
Parliamentary Under-Secretary of State,
Department of the Environment

29th July 1996

(a) S.I. 1987/1971: relevant amending instruments are S.I. 1994/470 and S.I. 1994/1807.

EXPLANATORY NOTE

(This note is not part of the Order)

Under section 9 of the Asylum and Immigration Act, the Secretary of State has power to specify classes of persons subject to immigration control for whom local housing authorities may provide housing accommodation (subsection (1)) or assistance under the homelessness legislation (subsection (2)). This Order specifies the following classes for the purposes of section 9(1) (article 3)—

Class A – a person recorded as a refugee;

Class B – a person who has been granted exceptional leave to enter or remain in the UK;

Class C – a person whose leave to enter or remain is not subject to any restriction;

Class D – an overseas student, in difficult to let accommodation let by a local housing authority to an education institution.

The classes specified for the purposes of section 9(2) are classes A to C above and (article 4)—

Class E – a person who claims asylum on arrival in this country or within 3 months of a declaration by the Secretary of State as to a fundamental change of status in his country of nationality if no determination has yet been made of the claim;

Class F – an asylum seeker in receipt of housing benefit on 4th February 1996 until the next decision on his claim is made.

IMMIGRATION

The Asylum and Immigration Act 1996
(Commencement No. 1) Order 1996
(SI 1996 No. 2053)

Made   *25th July 1996*

In exercise of the powers conferred upon him by section 13(3) of the Asylum and Immigration Act 1996 **(a)**, the Secretary of State hereby makes the following Order:

1.—(1) This Order may be cited as the Asylum and Immigration Act 1996 (Commencement No. 1) Order 1996.

(2) In this Order 'the Act' means the Asylum and Immigration Act 1996.

2. The provisions of the Act which are specified in Part I of the Schedule to this Order shall come into force on 26th July 1996; the provisions specified in Part II of the Schedule shall come into force on 1st September 1996; and the provisions specified in Part III of the Schedule shall come into force on 1st October 1996.

Home Office   *Ann Widdecombe*
25th July 1996   Minister of State

(a) 1996 c. 49.

Article 2   SCHEDULE A

PART I
PROVISIONS OF THE ACT COMING INTO FORCE ON 26TH JULY 1996

Provision of Act	*Subject matter of provision*
Section 3(3)	Appointment of special adjudicators
Section 3(5)	Procedure rules
Section 9(1) and (2), for the purpose only of making orders, and section 9(3)	Orders
Section 13	Short title, interpretation, commencement and extent

PART II
PROVISIONS OF THE ACT COMING INTO FORCE ON
1ST SEPTEMBER 1996

Provision of Act	*Subject matter of provision*
Section 2	Removal etc. of asylum claimants to safe third countries
Section 3, except subsections (3) and (5)	Appeals against certificates under section 2
Section 12, for the purpose of Schedules 2, 3 and 4 specified in this Part	Schedules
In Schedule 2, paragraphs 3(2) and 8 to 12	Amendments of the Immigration Act 1971
In Schedule 3, paragraphs 1, 2, 3 and 5	Amendments of the Asylum and Immigration Appeals Act 1993
In Schedule 4, the entry relating to the Asylum and Immigration Appeals Act 1993	Repeals

PART III
PROVISIONS OF THE ACT COMING INTO FORCE ON 1ST OCTOBER 1996

Provision of Act	Subject matter of provision
Section 4	Obtaining leave by deception
Section 5	Assisting asylum claimants, and persons seeking to obtain leave by deception
Section 6	Increased penalties
Section 7	Power of arrest and search warrants
Section 12(1) and (3) for the purpose of the provisions of Schedules 2 and 4 specified in this Part	Schedules
In Schedule 2, paragraphs 1(2) and (3), 2, 4 to 7 and 13	Amendments of the Immigration Act 1971 and the Immigration Act 1988
In Schedule 4, the entry relating to the Immigration Act 1971	Repeals

IMMIGRATION

The Asylum Appeals (Procedure) Rules 1996 (SI 1996 No. 2070)

Made   6th August 1996

Laid before Parliament   7th August 1996

Coming into force   1st September 1996

ARRANGEMENT OF RULES

PART I

Introduction

PART II

Appeals to special adjudicators

PART III

Appeals to Tribunal from special adjudicator

PART IV

Appeals from Tribunal

PART V

General procedure

SCHEDULE

Form A1 — Notice of an appeal to a special adjudicator against a refusal of asylum.

Form A1(TC) — Notice of an appeal to a special adjudicator against a certificate issued by the Secretary of State on third country grounds.

Form A2 — Application for leave to appeal to the Immigration Appeal Tribunal against a decision of a special adjudicator.

Form A3 — Application to the Immigration Appeal Tribunal for leave to appeal against its decision.

Form A4 — Recognizance of appellant.

Form A5 — Recognizance of appellant's surety.

Form A6 — Witness summons.

The Lord Chancellor, in exercise of the powers conferred by section 22 of, and paragraph 25 of Schedule 2 to, the Immigration Act 1971 (a) and now vested in him (b), after consultation with the Council on Tribunals in accordance with section 8 of the Tribunals and Inquiries Act 1992 (c), hereby makes the following Rules:

PART I INTRODUCTION

1. Citation, commencement and revocation

(1)   These Rules may be cited as the Asylum Appeals (Procedure) Rules 1996 and shall come into force on 1st September 1996.

(2)   The Asylum Appeals (Procedure) Rules 1993 (d) are hereby revoked.

2. Interpretation

(1)   In these Rules—

'the 1984 Rules' means the Immigration Appeals (Procedure) Rules 1984 (e);

'the 1971 Act' means the Immigration Act 1971;

'the 1993 Act' means the Asylum and Immigration Appeals Act 1993 (f);

'the 1996 Act' means the Asylum and Immigration Act 1996 (g);

'the appellate authority' means the special adjudicator or, as the case may be, the Tribunal and 'authority' shall be construed accordingly;

'appellant' includes an applicant and, where he appeals against the determination of the appellate authority, the Secretary of State;

'asylum appeal' means any appeal made under any of the subsections (1) to (4) of section 8 of the 1993 Act (including any further appeal that is made in

---

(a) 1971; section 22 was extended by the Asylum and Immigration Appeals Act 1993 (c. 23), sections 8(6), 9(4) and Schedule 2, paragraphs 4(3) and 5(4) and by the Asylum and Immigration Act 1996 (c. 49) sections 1(6) and 3(5).

(b) The Transfer of Functions (Immigration Appeals) Order 1987, S.I. 1987/465.

(c) 1992 c. 53.

(d) S.I. 1993/1661.

(e) S.I. 1984/2041.

(f) 1993 c. 23.

(g) 1996 c. 49.

relation to such an appeal) and shall include any appeal which, by virtue of paragraph 3 of Schedule 2 to that Act, shall be dealt with in the same proceedings as the appeal brought under any of those subsections and includes an appeal under section 3 of the 1996 Act;

'certified claim' means an appeal

(a) which the Secretary of State has certified is one to which paragraph 5 of Schedule 2 to the 1993 Act applies, or

(b) under section 3 of the 1996 Act (appeals against certificates under section 2);

'party' includes the appellant and the Secretary of State and, in cases where the appropriate notice is given, the United Kingdom Representative of the United Nations High Commissioner for Refugees;

'special adjudicator' means an adjudicator designated under section 8(5) of the 1993 Act or section 3(3) of the 1996 Act; and

'the Tribunal' means the Immigration Appeal Tribunal.

(2) In these Rules a Form referred to by letter and number means the Form so described in the Schedule to these Rules and any such forms (or forms substantially to the like effect) may be used with such variations as the circumstances may require.

(3) For the purposes of these Rules—

(a) an appeal is determined when written notice is sent of the decision whether or not the appeal should be allowed and expressions such as 'determination' and 'notice of determination' shall be construed accordingly;

(b) every determination shall consist of a concise statement of

(i) the decision on the substantial issues raised;

(ii) any findings of fact material to the decision,

(iii) the reasons for the decision.

3. Application

These Rules shall apply to all asylum appeals whether or not the appeal was instituted before these Rules came into force.

PART II APPEALS TO SPECIAL ADJUDICATORS

4. Application of Part II

This Part applies to asylum appeals to a special adjudicator.

5. Notice of appeal

(1) Subject to paragraph (2), a person making an asylum appeal ('the appellant') shall give notice of appeal not later than 7 days after receiving notice of the decision against which he is appealing.

(2) The time limit for giving notice of appeal shall be 2 days in a case where the following conditions are satisfied:

(a) the appeal is made under section 8(1) of the 1993 Act (where the appellant was refused leave to enter the United Kingdom); and

(b)   the appeal relates to a certified claim; and

(c)   the appellant is in custody in the United Kingdom, and

(d)   there has been personal service on the appellant of the notice of the decision against which he is appealing.

(3)   Subject to paragraphs (4) and (5), notice of appeal shall be given by serving—

(a)   on an immigration officer, in the case of an appeal under section 8(1) or (4) of the 1993 Act; and

(b)   upon the Secretary of State, in the case of an appeal under section 8(2) or (3) of the 1993 Act,
Form A1 which shall be

(i)   signed by the appellant or his representative; and

(ii)   accompanied by the notice (or a copy of the notice) informing the appellant of the decision against which he is appealing and the reasons for the decision.

(4)   In any case where an appellant is in custody, service under paragraph (3) may be upon the person having custody of him.

(5)   In any case where an appellant appeals under section 3 of the 1996 Act from outside the United Kingdom this rule shall apply to the appeal subject to the following modifications:

(a)   paragraph (1) shall have effect as if, for the words from '7 days after' to the end, there were substituted '28 days after the departure of the ship, aircraft, through train or shuttle train in which the appellant left the United Kingdom.';

(b)   paragraph (3) shall have effect as if, for 'Form A1', there were substituted 'Form A1(TC)'.

(6)   Where any notice of appeal is not given within the appropriate time limit, it shall nevertheless be treated for all purposes as having been given within that time limit if the person to whom it was given in accordance with this rule is of the opinion that, by reason of special circumstances, it is just and right for the notice to be so treated.

(7)   Upon receipt of the notice of appeal (whether or not the notice was given within the time limit), the immigration officer or (as the case may be) the Secretary of State shall send to the United Kingdom Representative of the United Nations High Commissioner for Refugees the documents specified in paragraph (3).

(8)   Within 42 days of receipt of the notice of appeal (whether or not the notice was given within the time limit), the immigration officer or (as the case may be) the Secretary of State shall send to a special adjudicator and the appellant—

(a)   the documents specified in paragraph (3);

(b)   the original or copies of any notes of interview; and

(c)   the original or copies of any other document (except statutory materials) referred to in the decision being appealed,
and, in a case where the time limit specified above has not been complied with, the Secretary of State shall notify the appellant and the special adjudicator why it has not been complied with.

(9)   In this Rule 'statutory materials' means any enactment or any provision made under an enactment, a convention or other provisions of a similar nature which are publicly available.

6.   Notification of hearing
Notice of the date, time and place fixed for the hearing of the appeal shall not later than 5 days after the receipt of the documents specified in rule 5(8) be served on—
    (a)   the appellant,
    (b)   the immigration officer or (as the case may be) the Secretary of State, and
    (c)   (if he has given notice in accordance with rule 8(2)) the United Kingdom Representative of the United Nations High Commissioner for Refugees.

7.   Variation of notice of appeal
The grounds of the appeal may, with the leave of the special adjudicator, be varied by the appellant.

8.   Parties
    (1)   The parties to an appeal shall be the appellant and the Secretary of State.
    (2)   If the United Kingdom Representative of the United Nations High Commissioner for Refugees gives written notice to the special adjudicator at any time during the course of an appeal that he wishes to be treated as a party to the appeal, he shall be so treated from the date of the notice.

9.   Deciding the appeal
    (1)   Unless the time limit is extended under rule 41, a special adjudicator shall decide an appeal not later than 42 days after receiving the documents specified in rule 5(8).
    (2)   The period specified in paragraph (1) shall be 10 days in a case where the appeal relates to a certified claim, except a certified claim in which the appellant appeals under section 3 of the 1996 Act from outside the United Kingdom.
    (3)   Where an appeal is remitted to a special adjudicator by the Tribunal pursuant to rule 17(2) or after an application for judicial review, the special adjudicator shall decide the appeal within 42 days of receipt of the Tribunal's determination or, as the case may be, of the appropriate court order.
In this paragraph 'appropriate court order' means the order made on the application for judicial review or the order made on any appeal against that order.
    (4)   Except where an appeal is determined without a hearing in accordance with rule 35 or summarily in accordance with rule 36, a hearing shall be held to decide an appeal.

10.   Adjournment of hearings
    (1)   Subject to rule 9(1) or (2), a special adjudicator shall not adjourn a hearing unless he is satisfied that an adjournment is necessary for the just disposal of the appeal.

(2)   When considering whether an adjournment is necessary, a special adjudicator shall have particular regard to the need to secure the just, timely and effective conduct of the proceedings.

(3)   Where a hearing is adjourned, the special adjudicator shall—

(a)   consider whether further directions should be given under rule 23, and

(b)   give notice either orally or in writing to every party to the proceedings of the time and place of the adjourned hearing.

11. Promulgation of determination and reasons

(1)   The special adjudicator shall wherever practicable pronounce his decision at the conclusion of the hearing and he shall not later than 10 days after the conclusion of the hearing send to every party to the appeal written notice of the determination.

(2)   In an appeal which relates to a certified claim, the special adjudicator shall, if he agrees that the Secretary of State was right to certify the claim, pronounce his decision at the conclusion of the hearing and he shall not later than 5 days after the conclusion of the hearing send to every party to the appeal written notice of the determination.

(3)   No notice sent under this rule shall be considered to be invalid by reason only of the failure to comply with any time limit prescribed.

PART III   APPEALS TO TRIBUNAL FROM SPECIAL ADJUDICATOR

12. Application of Part III

This Part applies to appeals to the Tribunal from the determination of a special adjudicator.

13. Leave to appeal

(1)   An appeal may be brought only with the leave of the Tribunal.

(2)   An application for leave shall be made not later than 5 days after the person making it ('the appellant') has received notice of the determination against which he wishes to appeal.

(3)   An application for leave shall be made by serving upon the Tribunal Form A2 which shall be—

(i)   signed by the appellant or his representative; and

(ii)   accompanied by the original or a copy of the special adjudicator's determination together with all the grounds relied on.

(4)   An application for leave shall be decided not later than 10 days after its receipt by the Tribunal.

(5)   Where the Tribunal fails to decide any application for leave under this rule within the time prescribed, the application shall be deemed to have been granted.

(6)   An application for leave shall be decided without a hearing unless the Tribunal considers that there are special circumstances which make a hearing necessary or desirable.

(7)   When an application for leave has been decided, the Tribunal shall forthwith send to the parties to the appeal a notice recording its decision on the

application for leave and, where leave to appeal is refused, the reasons for the refusal.

14. Notice of appeal

(1)   The application for leave to appeal shall be deemed to be the appellant's notice of appeal and may (as such a notice of appeal) be varied by the appellant with the leave of the Tribunal.

(2)   The Tribunal shall not later than 5 days after leave to appeal has been granted serve on the parties to the appeal notice of the date, time and place fixed for the hearing.

15. Parties

(1)   The parties to an appeal shall be the persons who were the parties to the appeal before the special adjudicator.

(2)   Where he would not otherwise be a party by virtue of paragraph (1), the United Kingdom Representative of the United Nations High Commissioner for Refugees shall be treated as a party to an appeal if he gives written notice to the Tribunal at any time during the course of an appeal that he wishes to be so treated.

16. Time within which appeal is to be decided

Unless the time limit is extended under rule 41, every appeal under this Part shall be decided not later than 42 days after the date of service on the Tribunal of the appellant's notice of appeal.

17. Deciding an appeal

(1)   Except where an appeal is determined without a hearing in accordance with rule 35 or summarily in accordance with rule 36, a hearing shall be held to decide an appeal.

(2)   Unless it considers—
    (a)   that it is necessary in the interests of justice, and
    (b)   that it would save time and avoid expense
to remit the case to the same or another special adjudicator for determination by him in accordance with any directions given to him by the Tribunal, the Tribunal shall determine the appeal itself.

18. Adjournment of hearings

(1)   Subject to rule 16, the Tribunal shall not adjourn a hearing unless it is satisfied that an adjournment is necessary for the just disposal of the appeal.

(2)   When considering whether an adjournment is necessary, the Tribunal shall have particular regard to the need to secure the just, timely and effective conduct of the proceedings.

(3)   Where a hearing is adjourned, the Tribunal shall—
    (a)   consider whether further directions should be given under rule 23, and
    (b)   give notice either orally or in writing to every party to the proceedings of the time and place of the adjourned hearing.

19. Promulgation of determination and reasons

The Tribunal shall record the decision on any appeal, and the reasons for it, and shall send to every party to the appeal, not later than 10 days after the conclusion of the hearing, written notice of the determination.

PART IV   APPEALS FROM TRIBUNAL

20. Application of Part IV

This Part applies to applications for leave to appeal, on a question of law, to the Court of Appeal or, in Scotland, to the Court of Session from a final determination of an asylum appeal by the Tribunal.

21. Leave to appeal

(1) An application to the Tribunal for leave to appeal shall be made not later than 10 days after the party seeking to appeal has received written notice of the determination.

(2) An application for leave shall be made by serving upon the Tribunal a notice of application for leave to appeal in Form A3 and the form shall be signed by the appellant or his representative.

(3) An application may be decided by the President or by a chairman of the Tribunal acting alone.

(4) The Tribunal shall decide the application without a hearing unless it considers that there are special circumstances which make a hearing necessary or desirable.

(5) The Tribunal shall decide the application, and shall send to the parties to the proceedings written notice of the decision and the reasons for it, not later than 10 days after the Tribunal has received the application.

PART V   GENERAL PROCEDURE

22. Application of Part V

(1) This Part applies to—

(a) proceedings to which Part II applies (appeals to special adjudicator);

(b) proceedings to which Part III applies (appeals to the Tribunal from special adjudicator);

(c) proceedings to which Part IV applies (applications for leave to appeal from the Tribunal); and

(d) applications for bail.

23. Conduct of appeals

(1) The appellate authority may, subject to the provisions of these Rules, regulate the procedure to be followed at hearings.

(2) The overriding objective shall be to secure the just, timely and effective disposal of appeals and, in order to further that objective, the authority may give directions which control the preparation for, and conduct of, any hearing.

(3) The authority may, after receiving a notice of appeal, give directions under this rule orally or in writing and notice of any written directions so given shall be served on all parties to the appeal.

(4)   Directions given under this rule may—

(a)   relate to any matter concerning the preparation for a hearing and, in particular, may specify the length of time allowed for anything to be done;

(b)   specify the place at which the appeal shall be heard;

(c)   in particular, provide for—

(i)   a particular matter to be dealt with as a preliminary issue;

(ii)   a pre-hearing review to be held;

(iii)   the furnishing of any particulars which appear to be requisite for the determination of the appeal;

(d)   require any party to the appeal to file—

(i)   statements of the evidence which will be called at the hearing specifying in what respect the services of an interpreter will be required;

(ii)   a paginated and indexed bundle of all the documents which will be relied on at the hearing;

(iii)   a skeleton argument which summarises succinctly the submissions which will be made at the hearing and cites all the authorities which will be relied on identifying any particular passages to be relied on;

(iv)   an estimate of the time which will be needed for the hearing of the appeal;

(v)   a list of the witnesses who will be called to give evidence;

(vi)   a chronology of events;

(e)   limit

(i)   the number or length of documents produced by, for example, requiring the appellant to specify to the respondent the passage or part of any document on which he will rely, especially if the document has to be translated into English for the hearing;

(ii)   the length of oral submissions;

(iii)   the time allowed for the examination and cross examination of witnesses by, for example, allowing a witness statement to stand as evidence in chief;

(iv)   the issues which will be addressed at the hearing;

(f)   facilitate the holding of combined hearings under rule 34.

(5)   The appellant and the respondent shall provide to every other party to the appeal a copy of any document which he is directed to file under paragraph (4).

(6)   Directions shall be given under this rule in an appeal in which the appellant is unrepresented only where the appellate authority is satisfied that the appellant will be able to comply with the directions.

24.   Failure to comply with directions

(1)   Subject to paragraph (2), where a party fails to comply with a direction given under rule 23 the appellate authority may—

(a)   treat that party as having abandoned the appeal or, as the case may be, treat the decision appealed against as having been withdrawn, or

(b)   proceed with the appeal; or

(c)   determine the appeal without a hearing under rule 35.

(2)   Where the appellate authority is satisfied that the party in default was prevented by circumstances beyond his control from complying with the direction given under rule 23, additional directions may be given under that rule.

25. Bail

(1)   An application by an appellant to be released on bail if made to—

(a)   an immigration officer or police officer, shall be made orally; or

(b)   the appellate authority, may be made either orally or in writing.

(2)   Where an application is made in writing pursuant to paragraph (1)(b), it shall contain the following particulars—

(a)   the full name of the appellant;

(b)   the address of the place where, and the purpose for which, the appellant is detained at the time when the application is made;

(c)   whether an appeal is pending at the time when the application is made;

(d)   the address where the appellant would reside if his application for bail were to be granted;

(e)   the amount of the recognizance in which he would agree to be bound;

(f)   the full names, addresses and occupations of two persons who might act as sureties for the appellant if his application for bail were to be granted, and the amounts of the recognizance in which those persons might agree to be bound; and

(g)   the grounds on which the application is made and, where a previous application has been refused, full particulars of the change in circumstances which has occurred since that refusal.

(3)   An application made in writing pursuant to paragraph (1)(b) shall be signed by the appellant or by a person duly authorised by him in that behalf or, in the case of an appellant who is a minor or who is for any reason incapable of acting, by any person acting on his behalf.

(4)   The recognizance of an appellant shall be in Form A4 and that of a surety in Form A5.

(5)   Where the appellate authority directs the release of an appellant on bail and the taking of the recognizance is postponed under paragraph 22(3) or 29(6) of Schedule 2 to the 1971 Act, it shall certify in writing that bail has been granted in respect of the appellant, and shall include in the certificate particulars of the conditions to be endorsed on the recognizance with a view to the recognizance being taken subsequently, the amounts in which the appellant and any sureties are to be bound and the date of issue of the certificate.

(6)   The person having custody of an appellant shall—

(a)   on receipt of a certificate signed by or on behalf of the appellate authority stating that the recognizance of any sureties required have been taken, or on being otherwise satisfied that all such recognizances have been taken; and

(b)   on being satisfied that the appellant has entered into his recognizance, release the appellant.

(7)   Paragraphs (4) and (5) above shall not apply to Scotland, and in its application to Scotland, this rule shall have effect as if

(a) for paragraph (2)(e) and (f), there were substituted—

'(e) the amount, if any, to be deposited if bail is granted;

(f) the full names, addresses and occupations of such persons, if any, who offer to act as cautioners if the appellant's application for bail were to be granted;';

(b) for paragraph (6), there were substituted—

'(6) The person having custody of an appellant shall on receipt of a certified copy of the decision to grant bail and on being satisfied that the amount, if any, to be deposited has been so deposited release the appellant.'.

26. Representation

(1) In any proceedings on an appeal, a party to the appeal may act in person or be represented or may appear—

(a) in the case of the appellant, by counsel or a solicitor, a person appointed in that behalf by any voluntary organisation for the time being in receipt of a grant under section 23 of the 1971 Act or, with the leave of the appellate authority, by any other person appearing to the authority to be acting on behalf of the appellant;

(b) in the case of the Secretary of State or any officer of his, by counsel or a solicitor or any officer of the Secretary of State;

(c) in the case of the United Kingdom Representative of the United Nations High Commissioner for Refugees, by a person appointed by him in that behalf.

(2) A person representing a party to an appeal in accordance with paragraph (1) may take all such steps and do all such things relating to the proceedings as the person whom he represents is by these Rules required or authorised to take or do.

27. Evidence

(1) In any proceedings on an appeal the Tribunal may receive as evidence the summary made in accordance with rule 43 of any evidence received—

(a) by the special adjudicator in the course of the proceedings to which the appeal relates, or

(b) by a special adjudicator to whom the appeal has been remitted in pursuance of paragraph (3)(c)(i) below.

(2) If any party to the appeal wishes to adduce evidence before the Tribunal further to that to be received in accordance with paragraph (1) above, he shall give notice in writing to that effect to the Tribunal indicating the nature of the evidence; and any such notice shall be given—

(a) in the case of the appellant, with the notice of appeal or as soon as practicable after notice of appeal is given or is deemed to have been given;

(b) in the case of any other party, as soon as practicable after he has been notified of the appeal.

(3) In any proceedings on an appeal—

(a) the Tribunal may, in its discretion, receive or decline to receive further evidence of which notice has been given in accordance with paragraph (2);

(b) if, to enable it to arrive at a proper determination of the appeal, the Tribunal requests the furnishing of further evidence relating to specified matters, it shall receive such further evidence;

(c) where such further evidence as is mentioned in sub-paragraph (a) or (b) falls to be received it shall be given, as the Tribunal may direct, either

(i) orally, in which case the Tribunal may take the further evidence itself or remit the appeal to the same or another adjudicator for the taking of that evidence, or

(ii) in writing, in which case it shall be given in such manner and at such time as the Tribunal may require.

28. Summoning of witnesses

(1) Subject to paragraph (2), the appellate authority may, for the purposes of any appeal, by summons in Form A6 require any person in the United Kingdom to attend as a witness at a hearing of the appeal at such time and place as may be specified in the form and, subject to the provisions of rule 29(2), at the hearing to answer any questions or produce any documents in his custody or under his control which relate to any matter in question in the appeal.

(2) No person shall be required, in obedience to such a summons, to travel more than 16 kilometres from his place of residence unless the necessary expenses of his attendance are paid or tendered to him, and when the summons is issued at the request of a party to the appeal, those expenses are so paid or tendered by that party.

29. Mode of giving evidence

(1) The appellate authority may receive oral, documentary or other evidence of any fact which appears to the authority to be relevant to the appeal notwithstanding that such evidence would be inadmissible in a court of law.

(2) In any proceedings before the appellate authority, no person shall be compelled to give any evidence or produce any document which he could not be compelled to give or produce on the trial of an action in that part of the United Kingdom in which the proceedings are conducted.

(3) The appellate authority may require any witness to give evidence on oath or affirmation, and for that purpose an oath or affirmation in due form may be administered.

30. Inspection of documentary evidence

(1) Subject to paragraph (2) below, when the appellate authority takes into consideration documentary evidence, every party to the appeal shall be given an opportunity of inspecting that evidence and taking copies if copies have not been provided pursuant to rule 23.

(2) Where on an appeal it is alleged that—

(a) a passport or other travel document, certificate of entitlement, entry clearance or work permit (or any part thereof or entry therein) on which a party relies is a forgery, and

(b)   the disclosure to that party of any matters relating to the method of detection would be contrary to the public interest,

then, if supply of a document to that party would involve such disclosure, that document shall not be supplied to, or made available for inspection by, that party.

31.   Burden of proof

(1)   If in any proceedings before the appellate authority a party asserts that a decision or action taken against him under any statutory provision ought not to have been taken on the grounds that he is not a person to whom the provision applies, it shall lie on him to prove that he is not such a person.

(2)   If in any proceedings before the appellate authority a party asserts any fact of such a kind that, if the assertion were made to the Secretary of State or any officer for the purposes of any statutory provisions or any immigration rules, it would by virtue of those provisions or rules be for him to satisfy the Secretary of State or officer of the truth thereof, it shall lie on that party to prove that the assertion is true.

(3)   In this rule 'statutory provision' means any provision contained in

(a)   the 1971 Act, the 1993 Act or the 1996 Act, or

(b)   any instrument made under those Acts,

and, in paragraph (2), 'immigration rules' means the rules for the time being laid down as mentioned in section 3(2) of the 1971 Act.

32.   Exclusion of public

(1)   Subject to the provisions of this rule, any hearing by the appellate authority shall take place in public.

(2)   Subject to the provisions of paragraph (4), where in accordance with section 22(4) of the 1971 Act (cases involving forgery of documents) the appellate authority is required to arrange for the proceedings to take place in the absence of a party and his representatives, all members of the public shall be excluded from those proceedings.

(3)   Subject to the provisions of paragraph (4), the appellate authority may exclude any member of the public or members of the public generally from any hearing or from any part of such a hearing—

(a)   at the request of a party;

(b)   where, in the opinion of the authority, a member of the public is behaving in a manner likely to interfere with the proper conduct of the proceedings and, to prevent such interference, that member or members of the public generally should be excluded, or

(c)   where, in the opinion of the authority, such evidence relating to a person other than a party is likely to be given as, subject to the interests of the parties, should not be given in public and no party requests that it be given in public.

(4)   Nothing in this rule shall prevent a member of the Council on Tribunals or of its Scottish Committee from attending a hearing in his capacity as such.

33. Hearing of appeal in absence of appellant or other party

(1) The appellate authority may, where in the circumstances of the case it appears proper so to do, hear an appeal in the absence of the appellant if satisfied that—

(a) he is not in the United Kingdom;

(b) he is suffering from a communicable disease or from a mental disorder;

(c) by reason of illness or accident he cannot attend the hearing; or

(d) it is impracticable to give him notice of the hearing and that no person is authorised to represent him at the hearing.

(2) Without prejudice to paragraph (1) but subject to paragraph (3), the appellate authority may proceed with the hearing of an appeal in the absence of a party (including the appellant) if satisfied that, in the case of that party, such notice of the time and place of the hearing, or of the adjourned hearing, as is required by rules 14(2) and 18(3) or, in the case of a hearing before a special adjudicator, by rule 6 and rule 10(3), has been given.

(3) The appellate authority shall proceed with the hearing in pursuance of paragraph (2) if the absent party has not furnished the authority with a satisfactory explanation of his absence.

(4) Where in pursuance of this rule the appellate authority hears an appeal or proceeds with a hearing in the absence of the appellant or some other party, it may determine the appeal on such evidence as has been received.

(5) For the purposes of this rule a reference to a party (including an appellant) includes a reference to his representative.

Combined hearings

Where in the case of two or more appeals it appears to the appellate authority that—

(a) some common question of law or fact arises in both or all of them; or

(b) they relate to decisions or action taken in respect of persons who are members of the same family; or

(c) for some other reason it is desirable to proceed with the appeals under this rule,

the authority may, after giving all the parties an opportunity of being heard, decide that the appeals should be heard together.

35. Determination without hearing

(1) An appeal may be determined without a hearing under this rule if—

(a) the special adjudicator has decided, after giving every other party to the appeal an opportunity of replying to any representations submitted in writing by or on behalf of the appellant, to allow the appeal; or

(b) the special adjudicator is satisfied that the appellant is outside the United Kingdom or that it is impracticable to give him notice of a hearing and, in either case, that no person is authorised to represent him at a hearing; or

(c) a preliminary issue has arisen and, the appellant having been afforded a reasonable opportunity to submit a written statement rebutting the respondent's allegation—

(i)　the appellant has not submitted such a statement, or

(ii)　the special adjudicator is of the opinion that matters put forward by the appellant in such a statement do not warrant a hearing; or

(d)　the parties agree in writing upon the terms of a determination, or

(e)　the special adjudicator is satisfied, having regard to—

(i)　the material before him;

(ii)　the nature of the issues raised; and

(iii)　the extent to which any directions given under rule 23 have been complied with,

that the appeal could be so disposed of justly.

(2)　Paragraph (1) shall apply with the necessary modifications to hearings before the Tribunal.

(3)　Where an appeal is determined under paragraph (1)(e), written notice of the determination shall be made available for public inspection.

(4)　This paragraph applies where—

(a)　the decision appealed against has been withdrawn or reversed by the respondent, and the special adjudicator is satisfied that written notice of the withdrawal or reversal has been given to the appellant by the respondent; or

(b)　the special adjudicator is satisfied, having regard to the material before him or to the conduct of the appellant or his failure to appear or otherwise to prosecute the appeal, that the appeal has been abandoned; or

(c)　the special adjudicator is satisfied, having regard to the material before him or to the conduct of any party, that the decision appealed against has been withdrawn.

(5)　Where the appellate authority is satisfied that—

(a)　the appellant was notified of the hearing date, and

(b)　the provisions of paragraph (4) apply to the appeal,

it shall send to the parties written notice that paragraph (4) applies (specifying the sub-paragraph which is appropriate) and it shall not be necessary to hold a hearing in order to determine the appeal or to issue a written notice of determination.

36. Summary determination of appeals

(1)　Subject to paragraph (2), where it appears to the appellate authority that the issues raised on an appeal have been determined—

(a)　in the case of an appeal before a special adjudicator, by the same or another adjudicator or by the Tribunal, or

(b)　in the case of an appeal before the Tribunal, by the Tribunal,

under Part II of the 1971 Act, under the 1993 Act or under the 1996 Act in previous proceedings to which the appellant was a party, on the basis of facts which did not materially differ from those to which the appeal relates, the authority may determine the appeal summarily without a hearing.

(2)　Before the appellate authority determines an appeal summarily in accordance with paragraph (1), it shall give the parties an opportunity of making representations to the effect that the appeal ought not to be so determined.

(3)   Where an appeal is determined summarily in accordance with paragraph (1), the appellate authority shall send to the parties written notice that the appeal has been so determined, and any such notice shall

(a)   contain a statement of the issues raised on the appeal and

(b)   specify the previous proceedings in which those issues were determined

and the provisions of rule 2(3)(b) shall not apply to such a notice.

37.   Performance of functions of Tribunal

The following functions may be performed by the President of the Tribunal or a chairman acting alone:

(a)   any function conferred on the Tribunal by Part II of Schedule 2 to the 1971 Act;

(b)   any function conferred on the Tribunal relating to applications for leave to appeal; or

(c)   any function conferred on the Tribunal of—

(i)   extending time limits under rule 41;

(ii)   remitting an appeal to an adjudicator pursuant to rule 17(2); or

(iii) requiring the attendance of witnesses at the hearing of an appeal.

38.   Notices etc

(1)   Any notice or other document required or authorised by these Rules to be sent or given to any person or authority may be sent by post or FAX or delivered, in the case of a document directed to—

(a)   the Tribunal, to the secretary of the Tribunal;

(b)   a special adjudicator, to any person employed as his clerk;

(c)   the Secretary of State, to the Appeals Support Section of the Asylum Division in the Home Office;

and, if sent or given to a person representing a party to an appeal in accordance with rule 26(1), shall be deemed to have been sent or given to that party.

(2)   A party to an appeal shall inform the appellate authority of the address at which documents may be served on him ('his address for service') and, until he gives notice to the authority that his address for service has changed, any document served at that address shall be deemed to have been served on him.

39.   Mixed appeals

(1)   This rule applies in any case where a person ('the appellant') is appealing to the appellate authority in relation to any of the grounds mentioned in subsections (1) to (4) of section 8 of the 1993 Act ('section 8 appeal') and is also appealing to the authority in relation to other grounds under Part II of the 1971 Act ('1971 Act appeal').

(2)   Where the appellant lodges his 1971 Act appeal before his section 8 appeal has been determined by the authority, the authority shall deal with both appeals in the same proceedings.

(3)   Where the appellant lodges his section 8 appeal before his 1971 Act appeal has been determined by the authority, the authority dealing with his section 8 appeal shall deal with both appeals in the same proceedings.

(4)   These Rules (so far as they relate to appeals to the authority) shall apply to the 1971 Act appeal as if that appeal had been a section 8 appeal and shall continue so to apply even if the section 8 appeal is determined before the 1971 Act appeal.

(5)   Nothing in paragraph (4) shall—

(a)   prejudice any steps taken under the 1984 Rules before the appellant lodged the section 8 appeal; or

(b)   require any step to be taken under these Rules which is analogous to a step already taken under the 1984 Rules.

(6)   The authority may adjourn a section 8 appeal or a 1971 Act appeal so far as is necessary or expedient for complying with a requirement in this rule to deal with both appeals in the same proceedings.

(7)   For the purposes of this rule, a person shall be taken to be appealing if he has given a notice of appeal in accordance with these Rules (in the case of a section 8 appeal) or in accordance with the 1984 Rules (in the case of a 1971 Act appeal) and, in either case, the appeal has not yet been determined.

40.   Transfer of proceedings

(1)   Where any proceedings before a special adjudicator have not been disposed of by him and the chief adjudicator, or any person for the time being carrying out the functions of the chief adjudicator, is of the opinion that—

(a)   it is not practicable without undue delay for the proceedings to be completed by that adjudicator, or

(b)   for some other good reason the proceedings should not be completed by that adjudicator,

he shall make arrangements for them to be dealt with by another special adjudicator.

(2)   Where any proceedings are transferred to another special adjudicator in accordance with paragraph (1)—

(a)   any notice or other document which is sent or given to or by the special adjudicator from whom the proceedings were transferred shall be deemed to have been sent or given to or by the first-mentioned adjudicator; and

(b)   any special adjudicator to whom an appeal is transferred shall have power to deal with it as if it had been commenced before him.

41.   Extension of time limit

(1)   Where under these Rules the appellate authority is required to decide or determine an appeal or to provide written notice of the determination at or within a time prescribed, the authority may if necessary extend the time so prescribed either to enable it fairly to make the decision or determination or (as the case may be) to provide the notice.

(2)   A special adjudicator shall not extend the time limit for giving notice of appeal except where it is in the interests of justice and he is satisfied that the party in default was prevented from complying with the time limit by circumstances beyond his control.

(3)   An extension may be made notwithstanding that the time limit in any case has already expired.

42. Time

(1) Subject to paragraph (2), any notice or other document that is sent or served under these Rules shall be deemed to have been received—

(a) where the notice or other document is sent by post from within the United Kingdom, on the second day after which it was sent regardless of when or whether it was received;

(b) where the notice or other document is sent by post from outside the United Kingdom, on the fifteenth day after which it was sent regardless of when or whether it was received; and

(c) in any other case, on the day on which the notice or other document was served.

(2) Where under these Rules a notice or other document is sent by post to the appellate authority, it shall be deemed to have been received on the day on which it was in fact received by the authority.

(3) For the purposes of these Rules, a notice or other document is received by the authority when it is received by any person employed as a clerk to the authority.

(4) Where under these Rules, an act is to be done not later than a specified period after any event, the period shall be calculated from the expiry of the day on which the event occurred.

(5) Where the time provided by these Rules by which any act must be done expires on a Saturday, Sunday or a bank holiday, Christmas Day or Good Friday, the act shall be done in time if done on the next working day.

(6) Where, apart from this paragraph, the period in question being a period of 10 days or less would include a Saturday, Sunday or bank holiday, Christmas Day or Good Friday, that day shall be excluded.

(7) In this rule, 'bank holiday' means a day that is specified in, or appointed under, the Banking and Financial Dealings Act 1971 **(a)** as a bank holiday.

43. Record of proceedings

A summary of the proceedings before the appellate authority shall be made.

44. Irregularities

Any irregularity resulting from failure to comply with these Rules before the appellate authority has reached a decision shall not by itself render the proceedings void, but the authority shall, if it considers that any person may have been prejudiced, take such steps as it thinks fit before reaching a decision to cure the irregularity, whether by amendment of any document, the giving of any notice or otherwise.

45. Correction of accidental errors

(1) Clerical mistakes in any determination or notice of determination, or errors arising therein from any accidental slip or omission, may at any time be corrected and any correction made to, or to a record of, a determination shall be deemed to

_____

(a) 1971 c. 80.

be part of that determination or record and written notice of it shall be given as soon as practicable to every party to the proceedings.

(2) The Tribunal may after consulting the special adjudicator concerned correct errors in a determination given by a special adjudicator and any correction made to, or to a record of, a determination shall be deemed to be part of that determination or record and written notice of it shall be given as soon as practicable to every party to the proceedings and to the special adjudicator.

6th August 1996   *Mackay of Clashfern, C.*

SCHEDULE

Form A1 — Notice of an appeal to a special adjudicator against a refusal of asylum

Notice of an appeal to a Special Adjudicator against a refusal of asylum

See Note 1 and Note 6 of the 'Notes' which are enclosed.

Asylum Appeal (Form A1)

Immigration Appellate Authority
Appeal Number:

Part 1: About you

Your surname or family name:

Your other names:

Your address:
Say where you are living now. If you are in a detention centre put its address.

Telephone number:
Give a number where you can be contacted during the day.

Your date of birth: Your nationality or citizenship:

Have you ever made **any other appeal** about Immigration?
    If you have put **Yes**:
    When did you appeal?

Put **No** or **Yes**:

The case number:
(if you know it)

What was the appeal about?

Part 2: Help with your appeal
(Your representative)
See Note 2 of the 'Notes' which are enclosed

Will anyone help you with your appeal?   Put **No** or **Yes:**
    If you have put Yes give:
    The person's name:
    Address:

Reference:

      Telephone number: FAX Number:

Part 3: The grounds of
your appeal

What is the Reference Number of the
Notice of Decision?
This number is on the cover of the Notice.

Why do you think the decision to refuse
you asylum was wrong?
If you need more space for your answer use another
sheet of paper and put your name on it.

Part 4: Declaration

See Note 2 of the 'Notes' which are enclosed.   I declare that the information I have
given is true and complete to the best
of my knowledge and belief.
I appeal to the Special Adjudicator
against the decision to refuse me
asylum.

*You, or your representative, **must sign.***   Signed: Date:

Are you the representative?   Put **No** or **Yes:**

Part 5: Documents you are sending with this form

See Note 4 of the 'Notes' which are enclosed.

Are you sending **any other documents** with this form (such as papers or photographs)?

> *If you have put* **Yes**:
> What other documents are you sending?
>
> *Please list the documents.*
> *See Note 5 of the 'Notes' which are enclosed. If you are providing an English translation of a document, include the original document and the translation in the list.*

■ The *Notice of Decision,* or a copy of it

*(You **must** send this document with the form)*

Put **No** or **Yes:**

Part 6: At the hearing of your appeal

See Note 3 of the 'Notes' which are enclosed.

At the hearing will you require an interpreter?

Put **No** or **Yes:**

> **If** *you have put* **Yes:**
> In which language?
>
> *Please give the dialect if you know it*

What to do next

You must now serve the form on an Immigration Officer, the Home Office or the person who has custody of you. Note 7 of the 'Notes' which are enclosed will tell you about service and where to serve this form.
Do not fill in any other parts of this form.

For use of the Home Office, Immigration Officer or Custody Officer

The appeal was received   at:

on:
at: [am][pm]

Who received the appeal?

How was the appeal received?   by hand ☐   by post ☐
The envelope is attached to this form.

Signed: Date:

For the use of the Home Office Appeals Support Section

Is the appellant in detention?   No ☐   Yes☐ The appellant is detained at

Signed: Date:

For the use of the Immigration Appellate Authority

The appeal was received   at:

on:
at: [am][pm]

Who received the appeal?

How was the appeal received?   by hand ☐   by post ☐
The envelope is attached to this form.

Signed: Date:

Notes about the   **Asylum Appeal (Form A1)**
Notice of an appeal to
a Special Adjudicator against
a refusal of asylum

Use the *Notice of an appeal* form if you have
been given a *Notice of Decision* and you want
to appeal against the decision.

1 When to appeal 🕒

You **must** give your appeal to the Home
Office, the Immigration Officer or the
Custody Officer within the time which the law
allows (see the Notice of Decision or Rule 5
of the Asylum Appeals (Procedure) Rules
1996).
Warning: the time may be as little as
2 working days.

2 Help with your appeal
(Your representative)

Someone may help you prepare your appeal
and they may fill in the form for you. You, or
your representative, **must** sign Part 4 of the
form.
Your representative may be anyone who can
be a representative **by law** (see Rule 26 of the
Asylum Appeals (Procedure) Rules 1996).

3 Presenting your appeal

You may put your case to the Special
Adjudicator or your representative may do it
for you.
If you require an interpreter at the hearing
of your appeal, the Immigration Appellate
Authorities will provide you with one.

4 Sending other documents

You must send the *Notice of Decision,* or a
copy of it, with the *Notice of an appeal* form.
If you want the Special Adjudicator to see
other papers or photographs please send them
with the form, if you can. If you do not send
the documents with the form, send them as
soon as possible to:
The Immigration Appellate Authorities,
York House,
Dukes Green Avenue,
FELTHAM,
Middlesex TW14 0LS.

5   *Documents which are not*   If you provide any other documents to
    in English   support your appeal and these are not in
                                 English, you must provide **either**
                                         the documents in their original language
                                         and a translation of them in English. You
                                         must arrange for the translation.
                                 or the documents in their original language
                                         and a description in English of
                                         ■ what the documents are
                                         ■ what the documents say in general
                                         terms.
                                         If a document is long (for instance, a
                                         newspaper) you may provide a
                                         description in English of only those
                                         parts which support your case.

6   *What to do*   Fill in Parts 1, 2, 3, 4, 5 and 6 of the *Notice
                                 of an appeal* form. If you need more space
                                 use another sheet of paper and put your name
                                 on it.
                                 Keep these *Notes* and the *Notice of Change
                                 of Address or Representative* (see Note 7 and
                                 Note 8).

7   *When you have filled in*   You must serve the form on an Immigration
    the 'Notice of an appeal' Officer or the Home Office.
                                 Who to serve
                                 Who you serve depends on the section of
                                 the Asylum and Immigration Appeals Act
                                 1993 under which you may appeal. The
                                 Notice of Decision will tell you that
                                 section.
                                 ■ **If you may appeal under Section 8(1)
                                 or 8(4)** serve the form on an
                                 Immigration Officer. The address is on
                                 the *Notice of Decision.*
                                 ■ **If you may appeal under Section 8(2)
                                 or 8(3)** serve the form on the Secretary
                                 of State for the Home Department. The
                                 address is on the *Notice of Decision.*

■ **If you are in custody** you may serve the form on the person who has custody of you.

Warning: Do not send the form and documents directly to the Immigration Appellate Authorities.

How to serve

You may serve the form by post, facsimile (fax) or by hand.

Keep a note of how you served the form, and when:

Served by: Post ☐ Recorded delivery ☐

Hand ☐   Fax ☐

Date: Time: [am][pm]

---

8   If you change your address or representative after you serve the form

If you change your address or your representative you must tell the Immigration Appellate Authorities and the Home Office. You may do this by

using the form *Notice of Change of Address or Representative*

or writing a letter. If you do this please make sure you give all the information which the form asks for.

You must send a copy of your letter, or of the form *Notice of Change of Address or Representative*, to the Immigration Appellate Authorities and to the Home Office. There is a copy of the form for each address.

If you have a representative

If you have a representative you must make sure you keep in contact with him or her. Letters about your case will be sent to your representative at the address you give until you or your representative tell the Home Office and the Immigration Appellate Authorities of any change of address or representative.

*Notice to the **Immigration Appellate Authorities** of a change of address or representative*

Asylum Appeal (Form A1)

About this form

■ If you change your address or your representative, you must tell the Immigration Appellate Authorities. Use this form to do that.

■ **What to do:**
Fill in Part 1, and Part 2 or Part 3 (or both Parts). Then send the form to: The Immigration Appellate Authorities, York House, Dukes Green Avenue, FELTHAM, Middlesex TW 14 0LS.
You may send this form by facsimile (fax). The FAX Number is 0181 831 3500.

Part 1: About you

Your surname or family name:
Your other names:
Your appeal or reference number:

*Please put **either**
the appeal number on letters sent by
the Immigration Appellate Authority
or the reference number on letters sent
by the Home Office.*

The appeal number on letters from the Immigration Appellate Authority:

The reference number on letters from the Home Office:

Part 2: Change of address

Your new address:
*Say where you are living **now**. If you are in a detention centre put its address.*

Telephone number:
Give a number where you can be contacted during the day.

Part 3: Change of representative

Your new representative's:
Name: _____
Address:

                                        Reference:
                                   _____
Telephone Number: FAX Number:

*Notice to the **Home Office** of*   **Asylum Appeal (Form A1)**
a change of address or representative

About this form

■ If you change your address or your representative, you must tell the Home Office. Use this form to do that.

■ **What to do:**
Fill in Part 1, and Part 2 or Part 3 (or both Parts). Then send the form to: The Appeals Support Section, Immigration and Nationality Directorate, Lunar House, 40 Wellesley Road, CROYDON CR9 2BY.
You may send this form by facsimile (fax). The FAX Number is 0181 760 1036.

Part 1: About you

Your surname or family name: _____
Your other names: _____
Your appeal or reference number: The appeal number on letters from the Immigration Appellate Authority:

*Please put **either***
  the appeal number on letters sent by
  the Immigration Appellate Authority
or the reference number on letters sent by   The reference number on letters from
  the Home Office.   the Home Office:

                                      _____

Part 2: Change of address

Your new address:

*Say where you are living **now**. If you are in a detention centre put its address.*

Telephone number:

Give a number where you can be contacted during the day.

Part 3: Change of representative

Your new representative's:
        Name:
        Address:

Reference:

        Telephone Number: FAX Number:

Form A1   Rule 5(3) The Asylum Appeals (Procedure) Rules 1996

Form A1(TC) Notice of an appeal to a special adjudicator against a certificate issued by the Secretary of State on third country grounds

Notice of an appeal to a Special Adjudicator against a certificate issued by the Secretary of State on third country grounds

See Note 1 and Note 6 of the 'Notes' which are enclosed.

Third Country Appeal (Form A1(TC))

Immigration Appellate Authority
Appeal Number:

Part 1: About you

Your surname or family name:

Your other names:

Your address:
Say where you are living now. If you are in a detention centre put its address.

Telephone number:
Give a number where you can be contacted during the day.

Your date of birth:

Your nationality or citizenship:

**Part 2: Help with your appeal
(Your representative)**
See Note 2 of the 'Notes' which are enclosed

Will anyone help you with your appeal?   **Put No or Yes:**
     If you have put Yes give:
     The person's name:
     Address:

Reference:

Telephone number: FAX Number:

Part 3: The grounds of your appeal

What is the Reference Number of the *Notice of Decision?*

This number is on the cover of the Notice.

_____

Why do you think the decision to refuse your asylum claim on third country grounds was wrong?

If you need more space for your answer use another sheet of paper and put your name on it.

Part 4: Declaration

_____

See Note 2 of the 'Notes' which are enclosed.

I declare that the information I have given is true and complete to the best of my knowledge and belief.
I appeal to the Special Adjudicator against the decision to certify my asylum claim on third country grounds.

*You, or your representative, **must** sign.*

Signed: Date:

Are you the representative?

Put No or Yes: _____

_____

Part 5: Documents you are sending with this form

See Note 4 of the 'Notes' which are enclosed.

■ The *Notice of Decision,* or a copy of it

*(You **must** send this document with the form)*

Are you sending **any other documents** with this form (such as papers or photographs)?

Put No or Yes: _____

> *If you have put* **Yes**:
> What other documents are you sending?
>
> *Please list the documents.*
> *See Note 5 of the 'Notes' which are enclosed. If you are providing an English translation of a document, include the original document and the translation in the list.*

_____

**Part 6: At the hearing of
        your appeal**
See Note 3 of the 'Notes' which are enclosed.

At the hearing will an interpreter
be required?

                                 Put **No** or **Yes:**

If *you have put* **Yes:**
In which language?
Please give the dialect if you know it

What to do next
                                   You must now serve the form on the
Home Office or the person who has
custody of you. Note 7 of the 'Notes'
which are enclosed.
**Do not fill in any other parts of this
form.**

**For use of the Home Office,
Immigration Officer or Custody
Officer**

The appeal was received   at:

                                    on:
                                    at: [am][pm]

Who received the appeal?

How was the appeal received?   by hand ☐   by post ☐
                                    The envelope is attached to this form.

                                    Signed: Date:

**For the use of the Home Office
Appeals Support Section**

Is the appellant in detention?   No ☐   Yes ☐ The appellant is
                                    detained at

                                    Signed: Date:

**For the use of the Immigration
Appellate Authority**

The appeal was received   at:

on:
at: [am][pm]
_____

Who received the appeal?
_____

How was the appeal received?   by hand ☐   by post ☐
The envelope is attached to this form.
_____

Signed: Date:

*Notes about the
Notice of an appeal to
a Special Adjudicator against
a certificate issued by the
Secretary of State on third
country grounds*

Third Country Appeal (Form A1(TC))

Use the *Notice of an appeal* form if
you have been given a *Notice of
Decision* which certifies your asylum
claim on third country grounds
and you want to appeal against the decision.

1   When to appeal ☉

You **must** give your appeal to the Home
Office, or the Custody Officer within the time
which the law allows (see the Notice of
Decision or Rule 5 of the Asylum Appeals
(Procedure) Rules 1996).
Warning: If you have left the United
Kingdom and you are appealing from abroad
you have 28 days within which to appeal.
If you are in the United Kingdom, you may
have as little as 2 working days in which to
appeal.

2 *Help with your appeal*
   (Your representative)

Someone may help you prepare your appeal and they may fill in the form for you. You, or your representative, **must** sign Part 4 of the form.

Your representative may be anyone who can be a representative **by law** (see Rule 26 of the Asylum Appeals (Procedure) Rules 1996).

3 *Presenting your appeal*

If the *Notice of Decision* states that you may appeal before you leave the country, you may put your case to the Special Adjudicator personally, or your representative may do it for you.

You may not put your case personally to the Special Adjudicator if you are appealing from abroad.

If an interpreter is required at the hearing, the Immigration Appellate Authorities will provide one.

4 *Sending other documents*

You **must** send the *Notice of Decision*, or a copy of it, with the *Notice of an appeal* form. If you want the Special Adjudicator to see other papers or photographs please send them with the form, if you can. If you do not send the documents with the form, send them as soon as possible to:

The Immigration Appellate Authorities,
York House,
Dukes Green Avenue,
FELTHAM,
Middlesex TW14 0LS.

5 *Documents which are not*
   in English

If you provide any other documents to support your appeal and these are not in English, you must provide **either**

the documents in their original language and a translation of them in English. You must arrange for the translation.

or the documents in their original language and a description in English of
■ what the documents are

■ what the documents say in general terms.

If a document is long (for instance, a newspaper) you may provide a description in English of only those parts which support your case.

6   *What to do*

Fill in Parts 1, 2, 3, 4, 5 and 6 of the *Notice of an appeal* form. If you need more space use another sheet of paper and put your name on it.

Keep these *Notes* and the *Notice of Change of Address or Representative* (see Note 7 and Note 8).

7   *When you have filled in the 'Notice of an appeal'*

You must serve the form on the Home Office. The Notice of Decision will give you the address.

If you are in custody in the United Kingdom and the Notice of Decision states that you may appeal before you leave the country, you may serve the form on the person who has custody of you.

How to serve

You may serve the form by post, facsimile (fax) or by hand where appropriate.

Keep a note of how you served the form, and when:

Served by: Post ☐ Recorded delivery ☐
Hand ☐   Fax ☐

Date: Time: [am][pm]

---

8   *If you change your address or representative after you serve the form*

If you change your address or your representative you must tell the Immigration Appellate Authorities and the Home Office. You may do this by

using the form *Notice of Change of Address or Representative*

or writing a letter. If you do this please make sure you give all the information which the form asks for.

You must send a copy of your letter, or of the form *Notice of Change of Address or*

Representative, to the Immigration Appellate Authorities and to the Home Office. There is a copy of the form for each address.

If you have a representative

If you have a representative you must make sure you keep in contact with him or her. Letters about your case will be sent to your representative at the address you give until you or your representative tell the Home Office and the Immigration Appellate Authorities of any change of address or representative.

*Notice to the **Immigration Appellate Authorities** of a change of address or representative*

Third Country Appeal (Form A1(TC))

About this form

■ If you change your address or your representative, you must tell the Immigration Appellate Authorities. Use this form to do that.

■ **What to do:**
Fill in Part 1, and Part 2 or Part 3 (or both Parts). Then send the form to: The Immigration Appellate Authorities, York House, Dukes Green Avenue, FELTHAM, Middlesex TW 14 0LS.
You may send this form by facsimile (fax). The FAX Number is 0181 831 3500.

Part 1: About you

Your surname or family name:

Your other names:

Your appeal or reference number:

*Please put **either**
the appeal number on letters sent by
the Immigration Appellate Authority
or the reference number on letters sent
by the Home Office.*

The appeal number on letters from the Immigration Appellate Authority:

The reference number on letters from the Home Office:

Part 2: Change of address

Your new address:

*Say where you are living **now**. If you are in a
detention centre put its address.*

Telephone number:

*Give a number where you can be contacted
during the day.*

Part 3: Change of representative

Your new representative's:
      Name:
      Address:

Reference:

Telephone Number: FAX Number:

*Notice to the **Home Office** of
a change of address or
representative*

Third Country Appeal (Form A1(TC))

About this form

■ If you change your address or your
representative, you must tell the
Home Office. Use this form to do
that.

■ **What to do:**
Fill in Part 1, and Part 2 or Part 3
(or both Parts). Then send the form
to: The Appeals Support Section,
Immigration and Nationality
Directorate, Lunar House,
40 Wellesley Road, CROYDON
CR9 2BY.
You may send this form by
facsimile (fax). The FAX Number
is 0181 760 1036.

Part 1: About you

Your surname or family name: _____

Your other names: _____

Your appeal or reference number:

*Please put **either***
  the appeal number on letters sent by
  the Immigration Appellate Authority
or the reference number on letters sent
  by the Home Office.

The appeal number on letters from the Immigration Appellate Authority:

The reference number on letters from the Home Office:

_____

Part 2: Change of address

Your new address:

*Say where you are living **now**. If you are in a detention centre put its address.*

_____

Telephone number:

Give a number where you can be contacted during the day.

Part 3: Change of representative

_____

Your new representative's:

      Name:

      Address:

_____

_____ **Reference:**

      Telephone Number: FAX Number:

Form A1(TC)   Rule 5(5) The Asylum Appeals (Procedure) Rules 1996

Form A2 — Application for leave to appeal to the Immigration Appeal Tribunal
against a decision of a special adjudicator

Application for leave to appeal to the Immigration Appeal Tribunal against a decision of a Special Adjudicator

Asylum Appeal (Form 2)

Immigration Appellate Authority Appeal Number:

■ *Please put the Appeal Number in the box opposite >*
This number is on the Special Adjudicator's decision.
■ *See Note 1 and Note 6 of the 'Notes' which are enclosed.*

Part 1: About you

Your surname or family name:

Your other names:

Your address:
Say where you are living now. If you are in a detention centre put its address.

Telephone number:
Give a number where you can be contacted during the day.

Your date of birth:

Your nationality or citizenship:

Have you ever applied for leave to appeal, or appealed, to the Tribunal?

Put **No** or **Yes**

If you have put **Yes:**
When did you apply for leave to appeal, or appeal?

The case number:
(if you know it)

What was the application, or the appeal, about?

Part 2: Help with your appeal
(Your representative)

See Note 2 of the 'Notes' which are enclosed

Will anyone help you with your appeal?   Put **No** or **Yes:** _____

     *If you have put **Yes** give:*
     The person's name: _____
     Address:

Reference: _____

Telephone number: FAX Number: _____

Part 3: The grounds of
your appeal

Why do you think the Special
Adjudicator's decision was wrong?

*If you need more space for your answer use another
sheet of paper and put your name on it.*

Warning:
*You must complete this section **now**.*
*Remember that you must send **at the same time:***
     this form with all parts completed
***and** all papers and photographs which you use to*
     support the grounds that you put in this part
     of the form.
See Note 4 of the 'Notes'.

Part 4: Declaration

See Note 2 of the 'Notes' which are enclosed.

I declare that the information I have
given is true and complete to the best
of my knowledge and belief.
I appeal for leave to appeal to the
Immigration Appeal Tribunal against
the Special Adjudicator's decision.

*You, or your representative, **must** sign.*   Signed: Date:

Are you the representative?   Put **No** or **Yes:** _____

**Part 5: Documents you are
sending with this form**

See Note 4 of the 'Notes' which are enclosed.

■ The *Notice of Decision,* or a copy of it.

(You must send this document with the form)

Are you sending **any other documents** with this form (such as papers or photographs)?

Put **No** or **Yes:**

> *If you have put Yes*:
> What other documents are you sending?
>
> *Please list the documents.
> See Note 5 of the 'Notes' which are enclosed. If you are providing an English translation of a document, include the original document and the translation in the list.*

What to do next

You must now serve the form. See Note 7 of the 'Notes' which are enclosed.

Do not fill in any other parts of this form.

**For use of Immigration
Appeal Tribunal**

The application was received

on:

at: [am][pm]

Who received the application?

How was the application received?

by hand ☐   by post ☐
The envelope is attached to this form.

Signed: Date:

Asylum Appeal (Form A2)

***Notes** about the Application for leave to appeal to the Immigration Appeal Tribunal against a decision of a Special Adjudicator*

If you want to appeal to the Immigration Appeal Tribunal against a decision of a Special Adjudicator, you must first get permission to appeal. This is called leave to appeal. Use this application form to apply for leave to appeal.
But you have no right to apply for leave to appeal if the Special Adjudicator has agreed with a certificate issued by the Secretary of State.

1 When to apply ◷

You **must** apply for leave to appeal to the Immigration Appeal Tribunal within **5 days** of getting the Special Adjudicator's decision (see Rule 13(2) of the Asylum Appeals (Procedure) Rules 1996).

2 Help with your application (Your representative)

Someone may help you prepare your application and they may fill in the form for you. You, or your representative, **must** sign Part 4 of the form.
Your representative may be anyone who can be a representative **by law** (see Rule 26 of the Asylum Appeals (Procedure) Rules 1996).

3 Presenting your application

You may put your case to the tribunal or your representative may do it for you.

4 Sending other documents

You **must** send with the application form, **at the same time**:

the Special Adjudicator's decision or a copy of it.

and all other papers and photographs which you use to support the grounds of your appeal.

5 *Documents which are not in English*

If you provide any other documents to support your appeal and these are not in English, you must provide **either**

the documents in their original language and a translation of them in English. You must arrange for the translation.

or the documents in their original language and a description in English of
■ what the documents are
■ what the documents say in general terms.

If a document is long (for instance, a newspaper) you may provide a description in English of only those parts which support your case.

6 *What to do*

Fill in Parts 1, 2, 3, 4 and 5 of the application form. If you need more space use another sheet of paper and put your name on it.

Keep these *Notes* and the *Notice of Change of Address or Representative* (see Note 7 and Note 8).

7 *When you have filled in the application form*

You must serve the form.
Who to serve
You must serve it on:
The Chief Clerk
Immigration Appeal Tribunal
Thanet House
231 Strand
LONDON WC2R 1DA
You must serve the form on the Chief Clerk whether or not you are in custody.
How to serve
You may serve the form by post, by facsimile (fax) or by hand.

Keep a note of how you served the form, and when:
Served by: Post ☐ Recorded delivery ☐
Hand ☐   Fax ☐
Date: Time: [am][pm]

8 *If you change your address*
   or representative after you
   serve the form

If you change your address or your representative you must tell the Immigration Appeal Tribunal.

You may do this by
   using the form *Notice of Change of Address or Representative*
or writing a letter. If you do this please make sure you give all the information which the form asks for.

If you have a representative

If you have a representative you must make sure you keep in contact with him or her. Letters about your case will be sent to your representative at the address you give until you or your representative tell the Immigration Appeal Tribunal of any change of address or representative.

Notice of Change of Address or Representative

Asylum Appeal (Form A2)

About this form

■ If you change your address or your representative, you must tell the Immigration Appeal Tribunal. Use this form to do that.

■ **What to do:**
Fill in Part 1, and Part 2 or Part 3 (or both Parts). Then send the form to:
The Immigration Appeal Tribunal Thanet House,
231 Strand,
LONDON WC2R 1DA.
You may send this form by facsimile (fax). The FAX Number is 0171 583 1976.

Part 1: About you

Your surname or family name: _____

Your other names: _____

Your appeal number:

You will find the number on letters sent to you by the Immigration Appellate Authorities.

_____

Part 2: Change of address

Your new address:

*Say where you are living **now**. If you are in a detention centre put its address.*

_____

Telephone number:

Give a number where you can be contacted during the day.

Part 3: Change of representative

_____

Your new representative's:
          Name:
          Address: _____

                                        Reference:
                                        _____

          Telephone Number: FAX Number:

Form A2   Rule 13(3) The Asylum Appeals (Procedure) Rules 1996

Form A3 — Application to the Immigration Appeal Tribunal for leave to appeal against its decision

Application to the Immigration Appeal Tribunal for leave to appeal against its decision

Asylum Appeal (Form A3)

■ *Please put the Appeal Number in the box opposite >*
This number is on the Tribunal's decision.
■ *See Note 1 and Note 4 of the 'Notes' which are enclosed.*

> Immigration Appellate Authority
> Appeal Number:

Part 1: About you

Your surname or family name:

Your other names:

Your address:
Say where you are living now. If you are in a detention centre put its address.

Telephone number:
Give a number where you can be contacted during the day.

Your date of birth:

Your nationality or citizenship:

Have you ever applied for leave to appeal, or appealed, to the Court of Appeal or Court of Session (in Scotland), against a decision of the Immigration Appeal Tribunal?

Put **No** or **Yes**:

If you have put **Yes**:
When did you apply for leave to appeal, or appeal?

The case number:
(if you know it)

What was the application, or the appeal about?

Part 2: Help with your appeal
(Your representative)

See Note 2 of the 'Notes' which are enclosed.

Will anyone help you with your appeal?   Put **No** or **Yes:** ___

    If you have put Yes give:
    The person's name: _____
    Address:

Reference:
_____

Telephone number: FAX Number:
_____

Part 3: The grounds of your
appeal

Please say why you think the Tribunal's
decision was wrong

Remember that you can appeal:
■ *against only the final decision of the Tribunal.*
  The Notes explain the final decision.
■ *only because you think the decision was wrong*
  on a question of law.
If you need more space for your answer use another
sheet of paper and put your name on it.

Part 4: Declaration

_____

See Note 2 of the 'Notes' which are enclosed.

I declare that the information I have
given is true and complete to the best
of my knowledge and belief.
I apply to the Immigration Appeal
Tribunal for leave to appeal to the
Court of Appeal or Court of Session
(if the decision was made in Scotland)
against the decision of the
Immigration Appeal Tribunal.

*You, or your representative, **must sign.***   Signed: Date:

Are you the representative?   Put **No** or **Yes:** ___

_____

What to do next

You must now serve the form. See Note 5 of the 'Notes' which are enclosed. **Do not fill in any other parts of this form.**

For use of Immigration Appeal Tribunal

The application was received

on:

at: [am][pm]

Who received the application?

How was the appeal received?

by hand ☐   by post ☐
The envelope is attached to this form.

Signed: Date:

Notes *about the*   **Asylum Appeal (Form A3)**
Application to
the Immigration Appeal Tribunal for
leave to appeal against its decision

The Immigration Appeal Tribunal made its **final decision** when it agreed or did not agree with the Special Adjudicator's decision.
You may appeal against:
    only the final decision of the Tribunal
and only because you think that decision was wrong on **a question of law**.

If you want to appeal to the Court of Appeal (or Court of Session in Scotland) against the final decision of the Immigration Appeal Tribunal, you must first get permission to appeal. This is called leave to appeal. You apply to the Immigration Appeal Tribunal for leave to appeal.
Use this application form to apply for leave to appeal **in an asylum case**.

1 When to apply 🕘

You **must** apply to the Immigration Appeal
Tribunal within **10 days** of getting the
Tribunal's final decision (see Rule 21(1) of
the Asylum Appeals (Procedure) Rules 1996).

2 Help with your application
(Your representative)

Someone may help you prepare your
application and they may fill in the form for
you. You, or your representative, **must** sign
Part 4 of the form.
Your representative may be anyone who can
be a representative **by law** (see Rule 26 of the
Asylum Appeals (Procedure) Rules 1996).

3 Presenting your
application

You may put your case to the tribunal or your
representative may do it for you.

4 What to do

Fill in Parts 1, 2, 3 and 4 of the form. If you
need more space use another sheet of paper
and put your name on it.
Keep these *Notes.*

5 When you have filled in the
application form

You must serve the form.
Who to serve
  You must serve it on
    The Chief Clerk
    Immigration Appeal Tribunal
    Thanet House
    231 Strand
    LONDON WC2R 1DA
How to serve
  You may serve the form by post, by
  facsimile (fax) or by hand.

**Keep a note of how you served the form,
and when:**
Served by: Post ☐ Recorded delivery ☐
Hand ☐   Fax ☐
Date: Time: [am][pm]

---

6 After you serve your form

If you have a representative

If you have a representative you must make sure you keep in contact with him or her. Letters about your case will be sent to your representative at the address you give until you or your representative tell the Immigration Appeal Tribunal of any change of address or representative.

Form A3   Rule 21(2) The Asylum Appeals (Procedure) Rules 1996

Form A4 — Recognizance of appellant

Recognizance of appellant   **Asylum Appeal (Form A4)**

About you

Your name   _____

Your address

Give your address
during the appeal

Your undertaking

I promise to pay to the Immigration Appellate Authorities the sum of **£**   if I do not comply with the following conditions.

The condition[s] [is] [are] that

I appear before the Authorities at:

on

at   [am][pm]
or at any other place and time that may be ordered.

[and that]   I reside at

or at any other address that may be approved.

[and that]   I report to the police station at

every
between the hours of   and
beginning on

[and that]

Signed   Date
(Appellant)

For official use

The appellant was detained
because

Taken before me	on	at	[am] [pm]
	Signed	Hearing Centre	

Form A4   Rule 25(4) The Asylum Appeals (Procedure) Rules 1996

Form A5 — Recognizance of appellant's surety

Recognizance of appellant's surety   **Asylum Appeal (Form A5)**

About the appellant

The appellant's name

The appellant's address

Give the address during the appeal

About you (the surety)

Your name

Please put your surname or family name in CAPITAL LETTERS.

Your address

Your undertaking

About your undertaking

When you sign the undertaking below you agree to pay a sum of money if the appellant does not comply with the conditions which follow. If that happens, but you think you should not have to pay, you will be allowed to tell the Authorities why not. The Authorities may then order you to pay the whole sum, part of the sum, or excuse you from paying any money.

The undertaking

I promise to pay the Immigration Appellate Authorities the sum of £   if the appellant does not comply with the following conditions.

The condition[s] [is] [are] that

the appellant must appear before the Authorities
at:

on

at   [am][pm]
or at any other place and time that may be ordered.

[and that]

the appellant must reside at the address given on the appellant's recognizance or or at any such other address as may be approved.

[and that]   the appellant must report to the police station at

every
between the hours of   and
beginning on
_____

[and that]
_____

Signed   Date
(Surety)
_____

For official use

The appellant was detained
because
_____

Taken before me   on   at   [am] [pm]
_____

Signed   Hearing Centre
_____

Form A5   Rule 25(4) The Asylum Appeals (Procedure) Rules 1996

Form A6 — Witness summons

Immigration Appellate Authorities   **Asylum Appeal (Form A6)**

To   Immigration Appellate Authority
                                                          Appeal Number:
of

Witness Summons

You are summoned to be a witness at the appeal of

You must attend   at

                   on
                   at   [am] [pm]

[You **must** bring to the appeal
   the documents]

Warning   If you do not attend the appeal according to this
                     summons, you may have to pay a fine.

                     If you have to travel more than 16 kilometres from your
                     place of residence to the appeal, you may claim your travel
                     expenses from the person who asked for you to be
                     summoned.

[Notice   This summons does not oblige you to show a
                     document to anyone without the permission of
                     the Immigration Appellate Authorities].

About the appeal   The appellant has appealed against the
                         [decision] [action] [determination]
                         of

                         that

                         I am satisfied that your evidence is necessary.

                     Signed   Date
                     [President] [Chairman of the Tribunal]
                     [Special Adjudicator]

Form A6   Rule 28 The Asylum Appeals (Procedure) Rules 1996

EXPLANATORY NOTE

(This note is not part of the Rules)

These Rules provide the procedure to be followed in deciding appeals to special adjudicators arising from claims for asylum, appeals from special adjudicators to the Immigration Appeal Tribunal and applications for leave to appeal from decisions of that Tribunal. They replace the Asylum Appeals (Procedure) Rules 1993, and give effect to the provisions of the Asylum and Immigration Act 1996. Other changes are designed to promote the just, timely and effective conduct of proceedings by:

(a)   specifying the matters to be included in a written determination *(rule 2(3))*;

(b)   specifying conditions for the grant of adjournments *(rules 10, 18))*;

(c)   providing that the Tribunal should decide appeals itself unless there are special grounds for remitting them to special adjudicators *(rule 17(2))*;

(d)   giving special adjudicators and the Tribunal power to make directions governing the future conduct of an appeal *(rule 23)*.

Index